A

Thomas Cook are the experts in travel.

For more than 135 years our guidebooks have unlocked the secrets of destinations around the world, sharing with travellers a wealth of experience and a passion for travel.

Rely on Thomas Cook as your travelling companion on your next trip and benefit from our unique heritage.

Thomas Cook **pocket** guides

NICE

Your travelling companion since 1873

Thomas Cook

Written by Paul Medbourne
Updated by Kathryn Tomasetti

Published by Thomas Cook Publishing
A division of Thomas Cook Tour Operations Limited
Company registration No: 3772199 England
The Thomas Cook Business Park, 9 Coningsby Road
Peterborough PE3 8SB, United Kingdom
Email: books@thomascook.com, Tel: +44 (0)1733 416477
www.thomascookpublishing.com

Produced by The Content Works Ltd
Aston Court, Kingsmead Business Park, Frederick Place
High Wycombe, Bucks HP11 1LA
www.thecontentworks.com

Series design based on an original concept by Studio 183 Limited

ISBN: 978-1-84848-282-1

Series Editor: Lucy Armstrong
Project Editor: Maisie Fitzpatrick
Production/DTP: Steven Collins

Printed and bound in Spain by GraphyCems

Cover photography (Statue outside Hotel Negresco) © PCL/Alamy

CONTENTS

SYMBOLS KEY

The following symbols are used throughout this book:

address telephone website address
opening times public transport connections

The following symbols are used on the maps:

information office	points of interest
airport	city
hospital	large town
police station	small town
bus station	motorway
railway station	main road
tram stop	minor road
cathedral	railway

1 numbers denote featured cafés & restaurants

Hotels and restaurants are graded by approximate price as follows:
£ budget price ££ mid-range price £££ expensive

Abbreviations used in addresses:

av. avenue
blvd boulevard
espl. esplanade
pl. place (square)
prom. promenade

Head to the Port for outstanding food and views

INTRODUCING
Nice

Introduction

The undisputed queen and capital of the French Riviera, Nice is France's fifth largest city, with a permanent population of nearly 400,000 and over ten times that number of visitors annually. Nice-Côte d'Azur airport welcomes more international passengers than any other in France except Paris Charles de Gaulle. Nice began catering to overseas visitors before organised tourism was born and has seen it all, adapting in turn to the tastes of Victorian British aristocracy, *fin de siècle* Russian princes, Jazz Age American millionaires and today's city-breakers, backpackers and family holidaymakers. Tourism is more than Nice's life-blood, it's its raison d'être.

If there is a 'real' Nice, it's not immediately apparent. The ambience is not typically French, nor Italian, even though Nice was an Italian city until 1860 and still retains strong cultural ties to its Mediterranean neighbour. The general standard of food is excellent, and there are plenty of places where you can sample authentic Provençal and French *haute cuisine* at its best, but most of its eating places are geared to international tourist tastes. It enjoys a beautiful setting on the Baie des Anges, but has no sandy beaches of its own. The glamour of the *belle époque* and art deco can still be seen in its buildings, but today it has shed its air of exclusiveness. It has an eventful past and has attracted visits from many of the great names of the last 200 years. Some of its natives, such as Garibaldi, Masséna and Simone Weil, Holocaust survivor and first President of the European Parliament, have been prominent on the world stage. But Nice wears its history lightly.

The truth is that Nice is too laid-back to worry. Its most visible characteristic is a casual attitude to life – and it works hard to ensure that its guests are relaxed and entertained. It provides safe and lively streets, seemingly endless sunshine, a clutch of world-class galleries and museums, over 200 hotels, cuisine from all over the world and in every price bracket, vibrant nightlife and an excellent transport infrastructure. Whatever your age, budget or tastes, Nice wants you to enjoy yourself.

Relax by the waterfall of Le Château

When to go

Nice's mild climate makes it an excellent weekend destination throughout the year. You can easily take a dip in the Med anytime between May and October, but it's best to avoid the crowds and the sky-high summer prices (of both flights and accommodation) by planning your visit during May–June or September–October.

SEASONS & CLIMATE

For the first 100 years or so of its tourism history, Nice was famed as a winter resort. Its location between the Mediterranean and the sheltering Alpes-Maritimes ensures that winter is comparatively warm (the average is 12°C/53°F December–March, and it rarely falls below 5°C/41°F) and summer not too hot (peaking in July and August at an average 24°C/75°F, though on some days it can reach around 30°C/86°F). June and September are probably the best summer months for comfortable heat.

It rarely rains for long in Nice. October and November are the rainiest months, but with an average rainfall of around 110 mm (4½ in) this is still hardly a deluge.

Nice's year-round sunshine has made it a tourist magnet for 200 years

ANNUAL EVENTS

February–March

Carnaval de Nice The city's premier event (see page 12), held over two weeks at Lent and culminating in a grand parade and fireworks on the final Sunday. Ⓦ www.nicecarnaval.com

Festin des Cougourdons (Gourd Festival) A traditional festival with local folklore and decorated gourds, held in the Jardins des Arènes de Cimiez. Ⓦ www.cougourdon.com

April

Semi-Marathon International de Nice This half marathon is run along the promenade des Anglais in late April. A shorter children's race and charity race also feature. Ⓦ www.nicesemimarathon.com

May

Fête des Mai Music, picnics and folk dancing celebrate the arrival of spring in the Jardins des Arènes de Cimiez. Held on Sundays and holidays in May.

Cannes Film Festival Head to Cannes to rub shoulders with the glitzy and glamorous, at one of the chicest festivals on the Riviera. Ⓦ www.festival-cannes.fr

Grand Prix de Monaco Just 25 minutes by train from Nice, a day at Monaco's Grand Prix is a must for Formula 1 fans. Ⓦ www.formula1.com

June

Fête de la Musique Stroll through Nice's city streets on 21 June to enjoy various bands, acoustic musicians and street performers vying for attention during one of France's most electrifying evenings. Ⓦ http://fetedelamusique.culture.fr

Fête du Château Head up to the Colline du Château for locally

produced meats and cheeses, traditional ravioli, fruit wines and hours of rocking music. A Niçois favourite. Ⓦ www.feteduchateau.com
Fête de la Mer Fishermen celebrate St Peter's feast day, 29 June, with a mass in the Gésu church followed by a procession to the Ponchettes beach, where a boat is ceremonially burned.

July–August
Bastille Day 14 July is marked by fireworks on the promenade des Anglais – grab a picnic and head down early to secure your spot among the crowds on the beach.
Nice Jazz Festival This big open-air event is held for eight days in July in the atmospheric surroundings of the Arènes de Cimiez (see page 106). Ⓦ www.nicejazzfestival.fr
Les Concerts du Cloître This festival of chamber music follows on from the Jazz Festival at the end of July and extends for two weeks in early August (see page 106). Ⓦ http://concerts.hexagone.net
La Castellada Actors and musicians reenact the history of the Château (see page 77). Ⓣ 04 93 84 86 11

September
Fête du Port The streets surrounding the Port are closed off to traffic on the first Saturday in September and quickly fill with music, drinking and dancing. Traditional wooden fishing boats give free rides to the other side of the action. Ⓦ www.riviera-ports.com
Fête de Catherine Ségurane Defender and patron saint of Nice, local washerwoman Catherine Ségurane caused the Turks to abandon their 1543 siege of the city by flashing her bare bottom at them. Join the locals in their candle-lit procession in her honour through the Old Town on 7 September.

October

Fête de Ste-Réparate Nice's Old Town celebrates its patron saint day on the first or second Sunday in October with masses, processions, dancing and music.

December

Régates Internationales de Star de Noël Top-level competitors contend for France's most important sailing regatta title.
t 04 93 89 39 78 w www.cnnice.org

PUBLIC HOLIDAYS

Le premier jour de l'an (New Year's Day) 1 Jan
Pâques & Lundi de Pâques (Easter Sunday & Monday) 12 & 13 Apr 2010, 24 & 25 Apr 2011, 9 & 10 Apr 2012
Fête du premier mai (Labour Day) 1 May
Fête de la Victoire (World War II Victory Day) 8 May
Pentecôte & Lundi de Pentecôte (Whit Sunday & Monday) 23 & 24 May 2010, 12 & 13 June 2011, 27 & 28 May 2012
Fête nationale (Bastille Day) 14 July
Assomption (Assumption of the Blessed Virgin Mary) 15 Aug
Toussaint (All Saints' Day) 1 Nov
Jour d'armistice (Remembrance Day) 11 Nov
Noël (Christmas Day) 25 Dec

Public transport runs to Sunday schedules, and banks, post offices and public buildings are closed on these days. Many shops (but not generally restaurants) are also closed.

Carnaval in Nice

In Nice the traditional pre-Lent celebrations have turned into the Riviera's biggest tourist spectacle. The exuberant celebration of Carnaval (from Latin *carne vale*, 'goodbye to meat') was first recorded in 1294. By the 18th century the riotous street parties had given way to exclusive indoor masked balls, and Carnaval was in the doldrums. It took the imagination of local citizen Andriot Saëtone to revive the old carnival spirit and at the same time transform it into one of the greatest shows on earth. His Festival Committee organised the first modern Carnaval parade in 1873, with a presiding monarch, a straw puppet called King Carnaval I. So began the tradition of the Carnaval King, who reigns over the two weeks or more of festivities. In 1876 a Flower Parade along the seafront was added, accompanied by the elegant tossing of bouquets between the carriages of the gentry; this quickly developed into a free-for-all chucking of flower petals into the crowd. These days the people on each of the 20 floats throw an estimated 100,000 gladioli, roses, carnations and mimosas to onlookers.

Prominent cartoonists are involved in the design of the theme after which each King is named. The themes are often topical or satirical: 2009's theme was the King of Masquerades, while 2010 celebrates the King of the Blue Planet.

The entire festival lasts over two weeks. Although theoretically it should end on Shrove Tuesday, in recent years the grand finale has taken place three to four Sundays before Easter. On the opening Saturday afternoon King Carnaval makes his entrance at the head of 20 themed floats, followed by 180 revellers wearing 'big heads' of papier mâché, accompanied by street theatre and music groups and the first Battle of the Flowers (there are several others during the festival). The programme continues with almost daily processions until the last big afternoon parade, after which, in the evening, King Carnaval marches to the beach, where his reign ends as he is ceremonially burnt.

Parades circle the promenade des Anglais, passing the seafront by the back of the opera house, and head along the quai des Etats-Unis, looping the Jardin Albert 1er and then returning through the main viewing area back along the promenade. Viewing areas on the north and south sides consist of both banks of seating and standing zones. Admission to either is by ticket only, bought on the day from on-site machines or in advance from the tourist office (see pages 151–2) or online at the Carnaval website (www.nicecarnaval.com). Tickets can only be bought online up to 48 hours in advance. Rates for 2010 vary from €25 per person for a seat down to €10 for a spot in the standing enclosure. The 2010 dates are 12–28 February. For a full calendar of events, ask at the tourist office or see the website.

Life's one long parade at Carnaval time

History

Greek traders founded Nikaia, 'City of Victory', in the fourth century BC near the modern port, but the area had already been inhabited for hundreds of thousands of years, as the finds displayed at Terra Amata (see page 101) testify. When the Romans arrived in the first century BC they preferred to build their settlement, Cemenelum, on the hill that is now the middle-class suburb of Cimiez. The Greek port became the medieval town corresponding to today's Vieille Ville. Possession of the town passed to the Italian House of Savoy, and Italian Nizza only became French Nice in 1860 by the Treaty of Turin. Remnants of the Savoy era include the ruins of the old castle of the Dukes atop the Château hill and the citadel of Villefranche (see page 114).

Nice's harbour was unsuitable for large-scale commerce, and the city might have become a backwater if 18th-century British travellers hadn't discovered its greatest asset – the climate. By 1822 the expat community was large enough to fund the construction of its own seaside walk, the promenade des Anglais. With the coming of the railway the stream of visitors became a torrent and Queen Victoria's first visit in 1895 bestowed the ultimate seal of approval.

The Russian aristocracy also felt the need to escape their own winters, and by the 1880s were buying and decorating villas, gambling and spending fortunes. Following the Russian Revolution of 1917 Nice was full of suddenly impoverished noblemen. Today's most visible reminder of the Russian invasion is the splendid Orthodox Cathedral (see page 78). Just as Russian money dried up, wealthy Americans discovered the Riviera, and Nice became an expatriate capital of the Jazz Age. Belle époque style was succeeded by art deco, best evidenced in the 1927 façade of the Palais de la Méditerranée (see page 39).

Nice's civic reputation in the years after World War II was marred by an unhealthy combination of crime, municipal corruption and ultra-right-wing politics. The return of wealthy Russian visitors, following the fall of the Soviet Union (they are once again the city's top-spending tourist nationality), has brought with it suspicions of Russian Mafia involvement in local crime. Yet Nice continues to attract an ever-increasing number of visitors, and is home to the second busiest airport in France.

LOCAL HEROES

To name a *place*, an *espace*, a *Musée*, a *Lycée* and a *rue* all after one man suggests that the locals must think highly of him. André Masséna was born in Nice in 1758 and after a brief spell in the military settled down in Nice as a shopkeeper with a sideline in smuggling. He re-enlisted after the French Revolution and reached the rank of marshal at the age of 35, serving under Napoleon as one of France's outstanding commanders until 1811, when his attempt to capture Lisbon was thwarted by the British under the Duke of Wellington. He never again held a command or returned to Nice, dying in Paris in 1817. A brilliant commander, a looter on a grand scale and a notorious womaniser, Masséna was rated by his nemesis Wellington as 'the only French commander who gave me sleepless nights'. By contrast, fellow-Niçois Garibaldi is commemorated only in a *place*, a *rue* and a statue. But then, he only reunified Italy, whereas Masséna defended France – although, owing to the changing nationality of Nice, Masséna was born an Italian and Garibaldi a Frenchman!

Lifestyle

By the end of the 19th century, Nice was among the first cities in the world whose economy depended on tourism, and catering to the foreign visitor remains its number one business today. The result is a truly cosmopolitan and tolerant atmosphere.

If you look at the names in the phone book or at the façades of the buildings in the Vieille Ville, you could believe for a moment that you were in Italy. On the other hand, the official infrastructure – police, post offices, Palais de Justice, street names – is totally French, and the iconic images of French life – citizens hurrying by with an armful of fresh baguettes, old ladies walking poodles – are in evidence everywhere. But wherever you stroll or sit down in central Nice, the conversations you overhear are as likely to be in English (from both sides of the Atlantic), Russian or Spanish as in French.

Perhaps it's harder to spot the residents because they enjoy much the same lifestyle as the tourists and have the leisure to do it – 10 per cent of the population are students, 29 per cent are over 60, and many of these are retired. Visitors and natives share the same basic pleasures – eating, drinking, chatting, promenading, people-watching and window shopping, all against a glorious backdrop of sun and sea. It's not difficult to fit in – all you have to do is enjoy yourself.

Having said that, life is just that bit easier if you observe some of the local niceties. Don't forget to say *bonjour* to the shopkeeper and *au revoir* when you leave the shop; include a *s'il vous plaît* when you ask for something and a *merci* when you receive it. Call the waiter '*monsieur*'. Begin a conversation with your hotel receptionist or bus driver with a few words of French, however bad; once local honour has been satisfied, you will soon find the conversation turns into English.

Hanging out, strolling, eating and drinking are major occupations

Culture

Whether it's due to the wealth and refined tastes of its upmarket 19th-century visitors or the magnetism that the Côte d'Azur has always exerted on artists, or maybe in an attempt to demonstrate that it's more than just a great holiday resort, Nice and its environs offer an amazing number of top-class public art galleries and museums. If you're serious about art (particularly 20th-century art), you could spend four or five days taking them all in. Even better, since July 2008, it's been free to get into all of Nice's municipal galleries and museums. These include the worthwhile Musée Archéologique and Musée Franciscain (see page 98). Privately-owned museums, such as the Chagall Museum, still charge an admission fee.

The cream of the 20th-century selection includes the Musée Matisse in the Cimiez district (see page 99), the Musée National Message Biblique Marc Chagall just north of the city centre (see page 100), and MAMAC (Musée d'Art Moderne et d'Art Contemporain) near the Old Town, featuring a wide selection of international modern art (see page 98). Further afield, the Fondation Maeght at St-Paul-de-Vence (see page 136) is a treasure-house of over 6,000 works by Braque, Chagall, Léger, Kandinsky, Miró and others (although not all are on display at the same time), while the **Musée Renoir** (ⓐ Chemin des Collettes ⓣ 04 93 20 61 07) at Cagnes preserves the artist's studio as it was in the last days of his life. More wide-ranging collections are housed in the Musée des Beaux-Arts Jules-Chéret (see page 85), with priceless works of the 15th–20th centuries, and the Musée Masséna (see page 82), both to the west of the city centre.

Visitors with an interest in history and archaeology will want

Musée Matisse is one of Nice's cultural highlights

to see the Roman-era discoveries in the Musée Archéologique in Cimiez (see page 98) and the nearby Arènes (see pages 92–3), the prehistoric finds and reconstructions at Terra Amata (see page 101), and the history of the city catalogued in the Musée Masséna (see page 82). More specialist and farther out of town, but well worth a visit for the quality of its collections of oriental exhibits, is the Musée des Arts Asiatiques (see page 84).

The other main aspect of Nice's cultural life is music. As well as the famous Jazz Festival (see page 106), the summer months are rich in musical events, many of them free: June has its sacred music recitals in churches around the town, and in July a series of free concerts of Mediterranean and world music, under the collective name *Musicalia*, takes place at the open-air Théâtre de Verdure near the seafront on Wednesday and Saturday evenings. The same venue sees performances of opera and operetta in September, as does the Opéra de Nice (see page 77).

The *What's On* section of the **Nice Tourism** site (W www.nicetourism.com) gives listings and offers an online booking service for musical events.

Nice's outdoor activities are endless

MAKING THE MOST OF

Nice

Shopping

The few large department stores in Nice are found along avenue Jean Médecin, including the unmissable ochre façade of Galeries Lafayette, a branch of the renowned Parisian store, and two blocks further up the Etoile shopping mall (four floors of chain-store fashion shops), cafés, FNAC and a large branch of C&A. The avenue also sports a wide range of smaller fashion boutiques and businesses selling bags and leatherware.

The long, busy, pedestrianised zone of rue de France and rue Masséna, heading west from the top of place Masséna, is a bustling thoroughfare of small souvenir shops and individual fashion boutiques. Famous designer names congregate just to the south and west of place Masséna, near the Jardin Albert 1er, and heading back towards rue Alphonse Karr and rue Paradis.

As well as containing the city's most enticing markets (see below), the Old Town is crowded with small shops. Many of them are true specialists in everything from faïence and mosaics to handmade toiletries, chocolates and foodstuffs; others offer a general range of souvenirs aimed unashamedly at the tourist purse.

The markets in cours Saleya in the Vieille Ville are great places to browse. In the daily flower and produce market (see page 66) you can pick up dried flowers, enticing packs of herbs and spices and craft items, as well as improbably coloured candy and sweets and top-quality fresh produce for a picnic. The night market in the same location (late spring to early autumn only) offers a wide range of gift ideas, from the funky to the irresistibly tacky. On Mondays the market changes to *brocante* (bric-a-brac): goods on sale range from

The Marché aux Fleurs takes place on cours Saleya

USEFUL SHOPPING PHRASES

What time do the shops open/close?
A quelle heure ouvrent/ferment les magasins?
Ah kehlur oovr/fehrm leh mahgazhang?

How much is this?
C'est combien?
Cey combyahng?

Can I try this on?
Puis-je essayer ceci?
Pweezh ehssayeh cerssee?

My size is ...
Ma taille (clothes)/
ma pointure (shoes) est ...
Mah tie/mah pooahngtewr ay ...

I'll take this one, thank you
Je prends celui-ci/celle-ci merci
Zher prahng serlweesi/
sehlsee mehrsee

exquisite vases to battered but authentic *gendarme*'s caps (as well as a lot of absolute junk).

Before you get stuck into shopping, stop to think about how best to spend your time and money here. There are no heart-stopping bargains in Nice but, equally, commerce is too competitive to allow rip-off prices. Generally, the quality is good for the price, and in some categories it can be very good indeed. Nice's proximity to the perfumeries of Grasse and herb-growing areas of Provence ensures a wide offering of handmade perfumes, soaps and toiletries. Dried and fresh herbs are available in profusion and make good gifts in themselves. Olives and olive oil are another regional speciality, and Nice offers a tempting choice at a standard unmatched elsewhere on the Med (see specialist Oliviera, page 71). Colourful Provençal fabrics are sold everywhere, either by the length or made up as table linen or clothing. If you are seriously interested in antiques, the shops of the Quartier des Antiquaires (see page 72) are worth checking out, in addition to the Monday market in cours Saleya (see page 22).

When the weather is fine, Nice is the perfect place to picnic. Whatever you like to eat and drink, you'll find plenty of places to buy provisions. As in most French cities, you are never far from a small grocer's shop or *boulangerie* (baker's), and of course the markets offer superb produce. If you need to buy a range of everyday necessities it makes sense to use one of the small supermarkets – look for the names Monoprix (central, on avenue Jean Médecin), Casino and Intermarché (outlets along boulevard Gambetta on the western edge of the city centre and dotted regularly throughout the rest of the city). If you're travelling by car, the 140 stores of the Cap 3000 complex at St-Laurent-du-Var near the airport will satisfy your every shopping need.

Printed Provençal fabrics make great take-home gifts

Eating & drinking

You will never have trouble finding somewhere to eat in Nice. Even late in the evening on Bastille Day you'd be unlucky to have to walk more than a few yards before coming across a free table for two. Budget is not a limitation, either: Nice caters equally well for cheap snacks and gourmet dining, with an endless mass of mid-range eateries in between that all offer a uniform but reliable bill of fare – excellent pizzas, standard pasta and Italian dishes, *moules frites* (steamed mussels and french fries) and seafood. Restaurants cluster around the main focal points of tourist traffic: rue de France/ rue Masséna pedestrian zone, the Vieille Ville, the seafront and the streets around the railway station. Don't overlook the Port area, which is lined with excellent seafood restaurants and some lively bars. Asian cuisine is easily found in most of these areas, and Turkish and Middle Eastern establishments are not hard to find. Specifically vegetarian restaurants are few (see page 75 for one of the best, La Zucca Magica), but it's easy to find tasty meat- and fish-free pizzas and salads on any menu; higher-class establishments will nearly always offer vegetarian choices.

Choosing a restaurant a few minutes' walk away from the most

PRICE CATEGORIES
Based on the average cost of a three-course evening meal for one person, excluding drinks. Lunch will usually be cheaper, especially if you opt for the good-value *prix fixe* (set menu) option at lunchtime.
£ up to €20 **££** €20–50 **£££** over €50

Le Bistrot de la Réserve serves up gourmet food with sea views

crowded streets will usually knock a few euros off the bill, though the ambience may not be so vibrant. Seafood, plentiful and top quality everywhere, is generally more expensive than meat-based dishes. The higher-range restaurants tend to close earlier, by 22.30 or 23.00, but the mid-range pizza/pasta eateries in the main tourist locations will still be serving (and still crowded) well after midnight.

A half-pint of beer (*une pression*) will set you back about €3, more if the bar or café is upmarket enough to set out a few complimentary olives and peanuts with your glass. On the other hand, you can make one drink last all night without getting a sour look from the waiter – drinking is regarded as an accompaniment to conversation, not an end in itself. If cocktails are your tipple, opt for the bar of a smart hotel; the versions served in ordinary cafés can be poor imitations. Most restaurants will offer a selection of mainly French wines; the climate and cuisine are tailor-made for a chilled bottle or carafe of rosé, in which the local Provençal and Corsican vineyards excel.

Restaurant menus are usually *service compris*, meaning that service is included, but it is usual to reward good service with a tip of 10 per cent or so. Again, it's common courtesy to leave the small change behind after a drink in a café. Major credit cards are accepted pretty much everywhere, but you may need to spend a minimum amount (usually €15) to use them. The French smoking ban came into effect in 2008, meaning that all bars and restaurants are either non-smoking or have a regulated, and very separate, smoking area.

If you don't fancy a full sit-down meal, there are plenty of places where you can grab a quick bite to eat at any time of day. Nice has its own native fast-food options in *socca*, *pan bagnat* and *pissaladière* (see page 30), and you shouldn't leave without trying them. Take-away food in the shape of sandwiches, filled rolls, pizza slices and kebabs is ubiquitous.

Additionally, Nice is picnic heaven – fresh bread (and tempting pastries) from the *boulangerie*, cooked meats and cheese from the *charcuterie* and superb salads and fruit from the greengrocer's, or better still the morning market in the cours Saleya. Head to place Gautier, a central square opening out on the north side of the *cours*, to buy divine seasonal produce, as well as jams, cheeses and *tapenade* (a type of olive pâté) directly from local farmers.

◐ *Everything for a picnic, for sale at the* boulangerie

Salade niçoise *with all the trimmings*

There are some things you shouldn't leave without trying. Nice's best known dish is *salade niçoise*, a delicious summer option of tuna, eggs, anchovies, tomatoes and salad – the better the restaurant, the more elaborate the version. Served up in a roll as fast food it becomes *pan bagnat*. *Socca* is a simple snack consisting of an oven-baked pancake of chickpea flour and olive oil. *Pissaladière* is a thin pizza-like street food topped with fried onions, anchovies and olives (no cheese or tomato). If you want to try *bouillabaisse*, the south coast's traditional meal-sized fish stew, you'll need to find a restaurant that serves it, and even then you may be required to give up to 24 hours' notice.

USEFUL DINING PHRASES

I would like a table for ... people
Je voudrais une table pour ... personnes
Zher voodray ewn tabl poor ... pehrson

Waiter/waitress!
Monsieur/Mademoiselle, s'il vous plaît!
M'sewr/madmwahzel, sylvooplay!

May I have the bill, please?
L'addition, s'il vous plaît!
Laddyssyawng, sylvooplay!

Could I have it well-cooked/medium/rare please?
Je le voudrais bien cuit/à point/saignant
Zher ler voodray beeang kwee/ah pwang/saynyang

I am a vegetarian. Does this contain meat?
Je suis végétarien (végétarienne). Est-ce que ce plat contient de la viande?
Zher swee vehzhehtarianhg (vehzhehtarien). Essker ser plah kontyang der lah veeahngd?

Where is the toilet (restroom) please?
Où sont les toilettes, s'il vous plaît?
Oo sawng leh twahlaitt, sylvooplay?

Entertainment & nightlife

Nice's climate encourages open-air amusement. Enjoying a leisurely outdoor meal, relaxing with a drink or two, attending one of the open-air musical events such as the Jazz Festival or *Musicalia* (see page 20), taking in the night views over the Baie des Anges, the bustle of promenaders on the seafront, the antics of the street performers and the strains of the (mainly Eastern European) street musicians – for most visitors this is enough to fill an evening. However, that's not all there is to do in the city.

If the weather outside isn't great or you just fancy a quiet night watching a film, there are plenty of options in Nice. You can catch movies in English (with French subtitles) at these cinemas:

Cinéma Rialto ⓐ 4 rue de Rivoli ⓣ 04 93 88 08 41 or 08 92 68 00 41

CASINOS

If you're over 21 and can afford to lose a few euros, a casino provides great evening entertainment. Dress smartly to get past the doormen and take your passport with you for ID and then, after maybe playing a few of the slots, move on to the tables, for which there will be a small admission charge. You don't have to bet your shirt to enjoy the experience – the real entertainment is in watching the high rollers and rubbing shoulders with the Riviera's rich and (sometimes) famous. The serious action doesn't start until around 22.00, but you can pass the time in the bar or restaurant beforehand. Nice's two casinos, Casino Ruhl and Palais de la Méditerranée, are both on the promenade des Anglais (see page 81).

No one goes to bed early in Nice

Bus: 3, 7, 8, 9, 10, 14, 22, 52, 59, 94 200

Cinémathèque de Nice (see page 96) 3 espl. Kennedy
04 92 04 06 66 www.cinematheque-nice.com Tram: Acropolis

Le Mercury 16 pl. Garibaldi 04 93 55 37 81 or 08 92 68 81 06
Tram: Garibaldi

If your night isn't complete without dancing, there are plenty of discos and bars where you can get your fix, from clubs and piano bars to pubs and cafés with live music. Streets running off the seafront, the Old Town and the Port area are the best areas to check out. See www.nicetourism.com for up-to-date listings.

Sport & relaxation

SPECTATOR SPORTS

Football Nice's football team plays at the 18,000-seater **Stade du Ray** (Ⓐ Av. du Ray Ⓣ Tram: Comte de Falicone) in the northern suburbs. OGC Nice may not have the international presence of Riviera neighbours AS Monaco, but in recent seasons they have managed a respectable middle-league position in the French First Division. The French football season runs from August to May, with most matches played on Wednesdays and Saturdays. Crowds are small (12,000 for the local derby with Monaco) but the supporters' Gallic passion makes for a great atmosphere, and tickets are much cheaper than for English Premiership games. See Ⓦ www.ogcnice.com for more information.

PARTICIPATION SPORTS

Beaches There are 15 beaches along the Baie des Anges, public beaches as well as the private stretches reserved for guests of hotels. All of them have pebbles rather than sand, but this doesn't put off the thousands of sun-worshippers who flock here on summer days. Beaches that feature a children's play area include Miami, Neptune, Ruhl and Voilier. Neptune also has pedaloes for hire. If you like sand with your sea, take a short trip to neighbouring Villefranche-sur-Mer (see page 112) for a family-style beach or Beaulieu-sur-Mer (see page 121) for a more sedate resort.

Bird's-eye view of the Med

Swimming is enjoyable anywhere: the beaches get high EU ratings and are supervised by lifeguards, and the water reaches a very warm 25°C (77°F) in summer. You'll be able to find opportunities to pursue a wide variety of water sports on Nice's beaches.

Scuba diving Nice is where much of today's standard scuba equipment was invented by the Forjon family in the early 20th century, and it is still a good place to learn to dive. The **Centre International Plongée Raymond Lefevre** (ⓐ Boat on quai des 2 Emmanuel, in front of Brasserie La Goelette, east of the old port ⓣ 04 93 55 59 50 ⓦ www.cip-nice.com) offers a first-time supervised dive for beginners (called a *baptême*) as well as packages for more experienced divers. There is another city-centre location at ⓐ 2 ruelle des Moulins. Villefranche is another good centre for diving of all kinds.

RELAXATION

Pétanque A rather more relaxing sport is the quintessential French game of *pétanque*, otherwise known as *boules*. You can play *pétanque* on the beaches in Nice; at St-Paul-de-Vence (see page 132) the local tourist office can rent you a set of *boules* or set up a lesson with a local player. To see the experts at play, visit in July, when Nice hosts the **Europétanque d'Azur championships** (ⓦ www.europetanque-dazur.com) in the Jardin Albert 1er, in which over 500 local teams participate.

Walking You don't have to try very hard or travel very far to find enjoyable places to take a stroll around Nice. The hill of Le Château (see page 64) is perfect for a gentle walk and a breath of fresh air. For a longer and more invigorating hike, catch a bus to the hillside of Mont Boron (see page 94).

Accommodation

With over 12,000 hotel beds and more than 700 holiday apartments, plus a good selection of youth hostels, Nice has no shortage of accommodation, although much of it is at the more expensive end of the market. The cheapest hotels cluster around the main railway station, which entails a bus ride or a 20-minute walk to the sea and the Old Town; mid-price options are mainly located in the central boulevards, a reasonable walk from the seafront, shops and sights. The central seafront and its side-streets are mostly the preserve of luxury hotels. If you're travelling by car, you also have the option of a reasonably priced motel room near the airport. Whatever accommodation you have in mind, remember that the French take their summer holidays in late July and August: book well in advance for that period.

HOTELS

Unless you have booked an inclusive package, it pays to investigate thoroughly on the web; in addition to the many commercial sites, the tourist office offers listings and instant reservations at Ⓦ www.niceres.com, which also covers self-catering options. Listed below are a few recommendations, but there are many more good hotels to choose from.

PRICE CATEGORIES

Based on the average cost of a double room. Breakfast is always extra and often poor value; some hotels lay on a full buffet, others the bare minimum of coffee, juice and rolls. If your hotel is one of the latter, take your *petit déjeuner* at any pavement café.

£ up to €100 **££** €100–200 **£££** over €200

Hôtel Villa La Tour £ Hidden away on one of the Old Town's back streets near the flower market, this small hotel with 14 rooms oozes charm. ⓐ 4 rue de la Tour (Old Nice & the Port) ⓣ 04 93 80 08 15 ⓦ www.villa-la-tour.com Ⓝ Tram: Cathédrale-Vieille Ville

Albert 1er £–££ A 1930s building on the edge of the Vieille Ville, with great views of the city and the bay. The 72 sound-proofed rooms have lovely oak furniture. ⓐ 4 av. des Phocéens (Old Nice & the Port) ⓣ 04 93 85 74 01 ⓦ www.hotel-albert-1er.fr Ⓝ Tram: Opéra-Vieille Ville, Masséna

La Maison du Séminaire £–££ A former monastery to the east of Nice's Port with fabulous sea-facing rooms. There's a fresco-filled chapel and a library with an unusual selection of world texts. ⓐ 29 blvd Franck Pilatte (Old Nice & the Port) ⓣ 04 93 89 39 57 ⓦ www.maison-du-seminaire.com Ⓝ Bus: 20, 30

Hôtel Suisse ££ Set into the cliffside of the Château hill at the eastern end of the Baie des Anges and well placed for the Vieille Ville and the port. There are staggering sea views from 35 of its 42 rooms. ⓐ 15 quai Rauba Capéu (Old Nice & the Port) ⓣ 04 92 17 39 00 ⓦ www.hotels-ocre-azur.com Ⓝ Tram: Cathédrale-Vieille Ville

Hôtel Windsor ££ This hotel is stylish and unique without costing a fortune. Many of the rooms have been individually decorated by leading contemporary artists. ⓐ 11 rue Dalpozzo (Western Nice) ⓣ 04 93 88 59 35 ⓦ www.hotelwindsornice.com Ⓝ Bus: 3, 7, 8, 9, 10, 14, 22, 52, 59, 94, 200, 400, 500, 710, 720, 750

Villa Victoria ££ Central quiet location and helpful staff, with a shady

Villa Victoria, one of many 19th-century townhouse conversions

garden for relaxation. ⓐ 33 blvd Victor Hugo (Western Nice) ⓣ 04 93 88 39 60 ⓦ www.villa-victoria.com ⓝ Tram: Jean Médecin

Le Grimaldi ££–£££ Located near Nice's *zone piétonne* and main shopping areas, the Grimaldi is a comfortable choice for an indulgent city break. ⓐ 15 rue Grimaldi (Western Nice) ⓣ 04 93 16 00 24 ⓦ www.le-grimaldi.com ⓝ Tram: Jean Médecin

Hôtel et Plage Beau Rivage ££–£££ Renovated a few years back by architect Jean-Michel Wilmotte, Old Town's Beau Rivage was Matisse's home between 1917 and 1918. Just steps away from the flower market and the seafront, the hotel boasts 118 rooms and a private beach. ⓐ 24 rue St-François-de-Paule (Old Nice & the Port) ⓣ 04 92 47 82 82 ⓦ www.hotel-nicebeaurivage.com ⓝ Tram: Opéra-Vieille Ville

Hôtel Negresco £££ A Nice landmark since 1912 and the grand old lady of the Riviera, patronised over the years by the elite. All 121 rooms and

24 suites are lavishly and individually decorated, while the restaurant, Le Chantecler, is Michelin-starred (of course). ⓐ 37 prom. des Anglais (Western Nice) ⓣ 04 93 16 64 00 ⓦ www.hotel-negresco-nice.com ⓝ Bus: 11, 52, 59, 60, 62, 94, 98, 200, 400, 500, 710, 720, 790

Palais de la Méditerranée £££ The modern hotel and casino behind the 1930 art deco façade of its predecessor was reopened in 2004. Check out the gorgeous views from the sun terrace. ⓐ 13–15 prom. des Anglais (Western Nice) ⓣ 04 92 14 77 00 ⓦ http://palais.concorde-hotels.com ⓝ Bus: 11, 52, 59, 60, 62, 94, 98, 200, 400, 500, 710, 720, 790

SELF-CATERING

For stays of a week or more, especially if travelling as a family, consider renting a holiday apartment; many of the complexes are modern and very central, and the abundance of food outlets and markets makes self-catering easy. Prices often beat most mid-range hotels. Check out **Nice Pebbles** (ⓦ www.nicepebbles.com), a reputable local organisation offering high-quality rental apartments in Nice and along the Riviera. The **Nice tourist office** website (ⓦ www.nicetourism.com) has some other options.

HOSTELS

Auberge de Jeunesse (HI) £ This youth hostel, located on a hillside 4 km (2½ miles) out of town, has exceptional city views. It's open from from June to September and is by far the cheapest accommodation option. ⓐ route Forestière du Mont Alban (Eastern Nice) ⓣ 04 93 89 23 64 ⓦ www.hihostels.com ⓝ Bus: 14, 82

Nice Camélias (HI) £ Basic rooms perfectly positioned in Nice's bustling centre, equidistant from the city's main train station

THE NEGRESCO

Henri Negresco, Romanian-born director of the Monte Carlo Casino, decided he could trade on his excellent contacts with royalty and millionaires by creating the grandest hotel on the Riviera, a palace fit to house his superstar friends. The result was the 1912 pink and white confection by Edouard Niermans that has become a National Historic Building and an icon of Nice. The interior has a fabulous art collection, with some quirky touches, such as the carousel in the lobby and the gloriously tacky illuminated name sign outside.

and the Old Town. ⓐ 3 rue Spitalieri (Eastern Nice) ⓣ 04 93 62 15 54 ⓦ www.hihostels.com Ⓝ Tram: Jean Médecin

Villa Saint-Exupéry £ Although 3 km (2 miles) from Nice's centre, the Villa more than makes up for its location with its leafy terraces, bar, huge self-catering kitchen, free breakfast and internet. Undoubtedly the best budget option around. ⓐ 22 av. Gravier (Western Nice) ⓣ 04 93 84 42 83 ⓦ www.vsaint.com Ⓝ Tram: Comte de Falicon

CAMPING

The Nice tourist office lists some 21 campsites. There are none in Nice itself; the nearest location is Cagnes-sur-Mer, about 20 km (12 miles) from the centre of Nice via the A8 motorway, or 20 minutes by train. However, the campsite is located some way from the railway station, which is in the middle of town. A local favourite is **Camping Les Romarins** (ⓦ www.campingromarins.com) at Eze, perched above Cap-Ferrat and boasting spectacular views.

The grand old lady has become a Nice landmark

THE BEST OF NICE

TOP 10 ATTRACTIONS

- **Vieille Ville** Exploring the colourful streets and markets (see page 62)
- **Cathédrale Orthodoxe Russe St-Nicolas** The architecture and atmosphere of the Russian cathedral (see page 78)
- **Promenades** A summer evening stroll along the promenade des Anglais (see page 81) and quai des Etats-Unis. You're guaranteed a couple of hours of free entertainment
- **A meal in Cours Saleya** A leisurely outdoor dinner anywhere in this pedestrianised street – enjoy the food and the buzz around you (see page 66)
- **Musée Chagall** The famous artist's enigmatic masterpieces in Cimiez (see page 100)

Chaises longues along the beachfront

- **A walk around the Château hill** A great spot to cool off and admire the views of the Old Town and Port. Collect your picnic ingredients in the market on the way there (see page 64)

- **Tours** If you have limited time and want to take in as much of Nice as possible, jump on the hop-on, hop-off 'Grand Tour' or the shorter 'Petit Train Touristique' around the city. Children will love them both (see page 59)

- **Open-air music** Jazz or classical music at the Arènes de Cimiez (see page 106) or one of the free concerts of the *Musicalia* (see page 20)

- **Lunch at the Negresco** Spoil yourself at the Michelin-starred brasserie (see page 38)

- **The Port by night** Soaking up the lively atmosphere or dancing the night away in one of the quayside bars (see page 68)

Suggested itineraries

HALF-DAY: NICE IN A HURRY

If you're just calling into Nice on a longer Riviera holiday, or maybe catching some sightseeing during a business trip, concentrate on the Vieille Ville (page 62). Time your visit for the morning, so that you can experience the flower and produce market in cours Saleya (not Mondays) before heading up the side-streets and reaching place Rossetti for a visit to the cathedral and a well-earned drink or ice cream at Fenocchio's. Don't miss the House of Adam and Eve, the Chapelle Ste-Rita or the Palais Lascaris on the way.

1 DAY: TIME TO SEE A LITTLE MORE

If you have the afternoon and early evening as well, leave the Old Town at the Ponchettes exit from cours Saleya and take a walk along the seafront, beginning along the quai des Etats-Unis and continuing along the promenade des Anglais as far as the Hôtel Negresco. You could use some of the time to soak up the sun on the beach, or head up from the promenade into the pedestrian-only rue Masséna for some retail therapy or a meal at one of the area's excellent pizza and pasta restaurants.

2–3 DAYS: TIME TO SEE MUCH MORE

After the above whistlestop tour of the centre, relax the next day with a morning stroll on the Château hill and descend from there into the Port to marvel at the opulent yachts and enjoy some freshly caught seafood. From the Port it's not a long walk to MAMAC (see page 98) and its quirky pop-art collection. Use your remaining time for short bus rides to Cimiez for the Chagall and Matisse museums, the Roman remains and the Franciscan monastery (see pages 98–101), to the Russian Orthodox cathedral in the northwest of the town (see page 78), and a little further afield, to the Beaux-Arts or Asiatic Art museums (see pages 84 & 85).

LONGER: ENJOYING NICE TO THE FULL

You'll want to return to some of the places suggested in the 2–3 day schedule, by day and night, but a longer visit gives you time to explore other places along the Riviera, which is easy with the excellent train and bus services. Make Villefranche (page 112) and St-Paul-de-Vence (page 132) your top priorities.

You can catch the flower market in cours Saleya on any day except Monday

Something for nothing

You don't have to put your credit card into the red to enjoy Nice, and many of its best experiences come at little or no charge. A cup of coffee at an outside table may seem a little pricey in itself, but it buys you a seat all morning if you want, while passing performance artists, locals and tourists keep you constantly entertained. Sunshine, fabulous views and fresh air are free, and there's nowhere better to enjoy them than the Château park (see page 64). If you get too hot, stand close to the waterfall and let it spray you cool.

It costs nothing to walk along the seafront in the evening and take in the street life – from seriously competitive rollerbladers to African drumming groups – that the promenade and the beach attract like magnets. In fact, anywhere in central Nice is good for people-watching, especially the markets. Browsing antiques at the Monday morning market in cours Saleya is an enjoyable experience that costs nothing, and even if you decide to buy something, the process of haggling with the vendor brings its own free show into the bargain, as the entire gamut of human emotion and Gallic gesture are displayed.

Since July 2008, all municipal museums (except the Chagall museum) have been free to enter, all of the time. Other must-see sights that are permanently free of charge include the Orthodox Russian Cathedral (see page 78) and the Palais Lascaris (see page 68). You can enjoy *Musicalia*, free concerts of Mediterranean and world music, at the open-air Théâtre de Verdure (between the seafront and the Jardin Albert 1er) on Wednesday and Saturday evenings in July.

Musée Masséna (see page 82) is one of the many museums with free entry

When it rains

You'd be unlucky, even in winter, to be forced indoors by rain in Nice for more than a morning, but for days when even the Mediterranean looks grey, the city offers all kinds of escapes.

With over 60 museums and galleries in the vicinity, not to mention villas, churches and palaces, there's always somewhere to while away a few hours indoors. The star museums – Musée Chagall, Musée Matisse, MAMAC, the Beaux-Arts and Asiatic Arts museums – could all easily occupy a half day. If you're a cinema buff you'll love the Cinémathèque's screenings of old classics in all languages (see page 96). Bad weather can't spoil the indoor attractions of the Old Town either – its baroque churches, the cathedral, the Palais Lascaris – and it also provides the perfect opportunity to gaze at the bejewelled interior of the Russian Orthodox Cathedral.

As well as cultural attractions, the temples of commerce offer a very handy refuge from the weather. Browsing in the Galeries Lafayette or the Etoile shopping mall on avenue Jean Médecin could keep shopaholics happily occupied for an entire day, if you include a spot of lunch. Smaller shops also have more to offer than you think – several of the mosaics boutiques in the Vieille Ville invite you to try your hand at this fascinating handicraft. In the same area, Poterie Painting (see page 72) will show you how to create your own souvenirs by designing and painting your own pottery to take away with you. If you're looking for something more active, why not get wet anyway, in one of Nice's indoor swimming pools? The two most central are:

Piscine Jean Médecin ⓐ 178 rue de France ⓣ 04 93 86 24 01 Ⓝ Bus: 3, 8, 9
Piscine St-François ⓐ 13 pl. St-François ⓣ 04 93 85 53 08 Ⓝ Tram: Cathédrale-Vieille Ville

Browsing in galleries is a great way to escape the rain

On arrival

TIME DIFFERENCE

French clocks follow Central European Time (CET). During Daylight Saving Time (end Mar–end Oct), the clocks go forward one hour.

ARRIVING

By air

As your aeroplane descends into **Nice-Côte d'Azur Airport** (08 20 423 333 www.nice.aeroport.fr) you will get some wonderful views of the Côte d'Azur, as the runways are almost surrounded by the sea. The airport is the second largest in France in terms of passengers (over ten million a year), but it's a manageable size and gets its customers landside pretty quickly. In each of the two terminals there is a bank and bureau de change. The airport is just 7 km (4 miles) from the city centre. Buses run from outside Terminals 1 and 2, departing every 20 minutes and taking about 30 minutes to reach their destination. **Bus 98** (06.05–23.50) goes to the city's *gare routière*, or main bus station, and from mid-July to mid-September it also goes to the Port. **Bus 99** (07.50–21.00) goes to Nice-Ville, the city's main train station. The ticket, which you can purchase on board, is valid on all Ligne d'Azur buses until midnight. See www.lignedazur.com.

The local TER train will get you to Nice-Ville station in about six minutes, but, strangely enough, there's no bus transfer that covers the five-minute walk from the terminal to St Augustin, the airport's main station. If you are carrying luggage, it's easier to take the bus.

Taxis are also available, taking 30 minutes to reach the city centre and costing around €30. For about the same price you can pre-book a door-to-door minibus from **Airport Transfer Service**

The views start before you even land

(www.a-t-s.net four passengers minimum). If time is of the essence, then opt for one of the fast motorcycle-taxis; see www.jam-dodgers.com or www.rivieraxpress.fr for details.

By rail

The main SNCF railway station, **Nice-Ville** (also called Gare Thiers av. Thiers 04 92 14 82 52 www.sncf.fr), is situated on the northern edge of the city. The easiest way to reach the city centre is by tram: the station's stop is called Gare Thiers. There are also plenty of buses and taxis.

By road

Long-distance and international buses arrive at Nice's *gare routière* (central bus station), which is conveniently located just north of the Old Town. You can catch a number of local buses from here. A useful coach company operating in Nice is **Eurolines** (5 blvd Jean Jaurès 08 92 89 90 91 or 01 41 86 24 21 www.eurolines.fr).

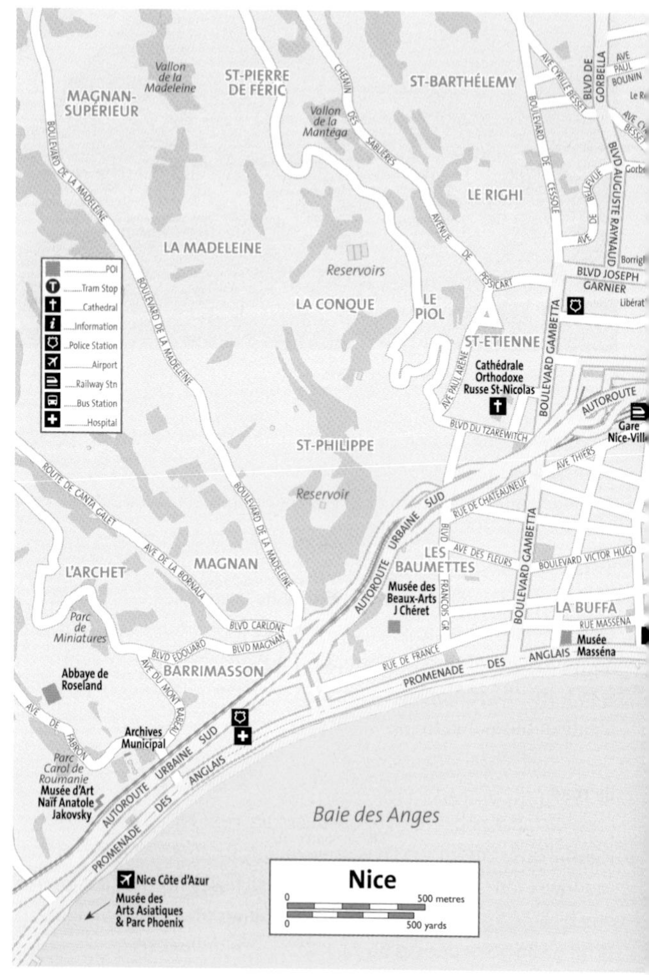
MAGNAN-SUPÉRIEUR
Vallon de la Madeleine
ST-PIERRE DE FÉRIC
Vallon de la Mantéga
ST-BARTHÉLEMY
LE RIGHI
LA MADELEINE
Reservoirs
LA CONQUE
LE PIOL
ST-ETIENNE
Cathédrale Orthodoxe Russe St-Nicolas
ST-PHILIPPE
Reservoir
MAGNAN
L'ARCHET
LES BAUMETTES
Musée des Beaux-Arts J Chéret
LA BUFFA
Musée Masséna
Parc de Miniatures
BARRIMASSON
Abbaye de Roseland
Archives Municipal
Parc Carol de Roumanie
Musée d'Art Naïf Anatole Jakovsky
Baie des Anges
Gare Nice-Vill
Nice Côte d'Azur
Musée des Arts Asiatiques & Parc Phoenix
BOULEVARD DE LA MADELEINE
CHEMIN DES SABLIÈRES
AVENUE DE PESSICART
AVE CYRILLE BESSET
BOULEVARD DE CESSOLE
BLVD DE GORBELLA
AVE PAUL BOUNIN
BLVD AUGUSTE RAYNAUD
AVE DE BELLEVUE
BLVD JOSEPH GARNIER
BOULEVARD GAMBETTA
AVE PAUL ARÈNE
BLVD DU TZAREWITCH
AUTOROUTE
AVE THIERS
RUE DE CHÂTEAUNEUF
AUTOROUTE URBAINE SUD
ROUTE DE CANTA GALET
AVE DE LA BORNALA
AVE DES FLEURS
BOULEVARD VICTOR HUGO
BLVD FRANÇOIS GR
RUE MASSÉNA
BLVD CARLONE
BLVD MAGNAN
BLVD EDOUARD
AVE DU MONT RABEAU
RUE DE FRANCE
PROMENADE DES ANGLAIS
AVE DE FABRON
POI
Tram Stop
Cathedral
Information
Police Station
Airport
Railway Stn
Bus Station
Hospital
Nice
0
500 metres
0
500 yards

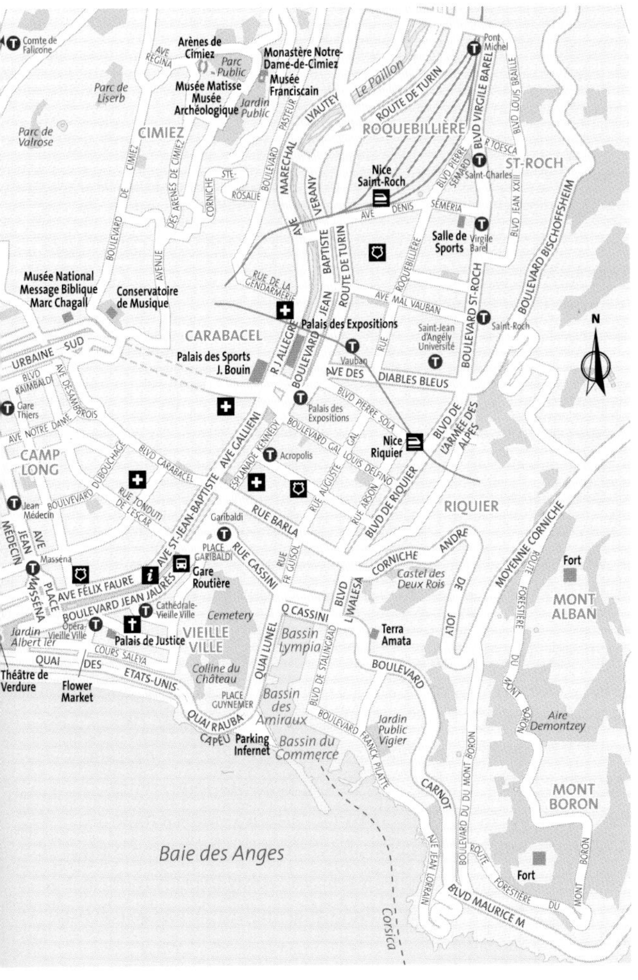
Comte de Falicone
Arènes de Cimiez
Parc Public
Monastère Notre-Dame-de-Cimiez
Musée Franciscain
Musée Matisse
Musée Archéologique
Jardin Public
Parc de Liserb
Parc de Valrose
CIMIEZ
Le Paillon
ROUTE DE TURIN
ROQUEBILLIÈRE
Pont Michel
BLVD VIRGILE BAREL
ST-ROCH
Saint-Charles
Nice Saint-Roch
Salle de Sports
Virgile Barel
Musée National Message Biblique Marc Chagall
Conservatoire de Musique
CARABACEL
Palais des Expositions
Saint-Jean d'Angély Université
Saint-Roch
BOULEVARD BISCHOFFSHEIM
Palais des Sports J. Bouin
Vauban
AVE DES DIABLES BLEUS
Gare Thiers
CAMP LONG
Palais des Expositions
Acropolis
Nice Riquier
RIQUIER
Jean Médecin
Garibaldi
PLACE GARIBALDI
Masséna
Gare Routière
AVE FÉLIX FAURE
BOULEVARD JEAN JAURÈS
Cathédrale-Vieille Ville
Opéra-Vieille Ville
Palais de Justice
Cemetery
VIEILLE VILLE
Jardin Albert 1er
Théâtre de Verdure
Flower Market
COURS SALEYA
QUAI DES ETATS-UNIS
Colline du Château
Bassin Lympia
Castel des Deux Rois
Terra Amata
Fort
MONT ALBAN
MOYENNE CORNICHE
Aire Demontzey
Jardin Public Vigier
PLACE GUYNEMER
Bassin des Amiraux
QUAI RAUBA CAPEU
Parking Infernet
Bassin du Commerce
MONT BORON
Baie des Anges
Corsica
Fort
BLVD MAURICE M
N

The A8 motorway skirts the northern edge of Nice. If approaching from the west, turn off at junction 50 either onto the *autoroute urbain sud*, the urban motorway, which will take you to the north of the centre, or follow signs to the promenade des Anglais to arrive at the seafront itself. Make sure you adjust quickly to slow-moving traffic and watch out for one-way systems as you approach the centre. It's a good idea to park as soon as you get near the centre. If you take the urban motorway, turn off towards 'Gare SNCF' and park at the avenue Thiers car park; there is a tourist office at the nearby railway station. If you arrive on the promenade, the first central car park you will see is near the Musée Masséna, 200 yards from the city's main tourist office.

By water

Nice's commercial Port offers frequent ferries to Corsica (Bastia, Calvi, Ile Rousse and Ajaccio). For information and timetables, check **Corsica Sardinia Ferries** (ⓦ www.corsicaferries.com) or **SNCM Ferries** (ⓦ www.sncm.fr). Both companies operate traditional slower car ferries (journey time approximately about five hours) and high-speed links (around three hours) to and from the island.

FINDING YOUR FEET

Once you've arrived, you'll find that the noise and traffic, though ever-present, are not as bad as in many Mediterranean cities. Although the only true pedestrian zones (*zones piétonnes*) are the Vieille Ville and rue de France/rue Masséna, many of the boulevards see little traffic. The main arteries – promenade des Anglais, avenue Jean Médecin and the roads flanking the central Paillon green space – are always busy. It's okay to cross the street at any point if there's no traffic (but check that you know which way it should be coming – most of Nice's roads are one-way).

Check out the personal safety tips on pages 145–6, although you are unlikely to feel threatened in central Nice at any time. Pickpockets are the danger you're most likely to encounter – get into the habit of keeping your bag or purse closed and within sight. Bring a map with you or get one from a shop or the tourist office as soon as you can; asking directions can be frustrating when half the people you meet are strangers to Nice as well.

Dress comfortably, and as casually as you like. However, the locals have a low tolerance of swimwear, and shirtless men, in the streets. Even the bus station displays a warning against 'unsuitable attire'. Save it for the beach or your hotel balcony.

IF YOU GET LOST, TRY ...

Excuse me, do you speak English?
Excusez-moi, vous parlez anglais?
Ekskeweh mwah, voopahrlay ahnglay?

Excuse me, is this the right way to the Old Town/the city centre/the tourist office/the station/the bus station?
Excusez-moi, c'est la bonne direction pour la vieille ville/le centre-ville/l'office de tourisme/la gare/la gare routière?
Ekskewzaymwah, seh lah bon deerekseeawng poor lah veeay veel/leh sahngtr veel/lohfeece de tooreezm/lah gahr/lah gahr rootyair?

Can you point to it on my map?
Pourriez-vous me le montrer sur la carte?
Pooreehvoo mer ler mawngtreh sewr lah kart?

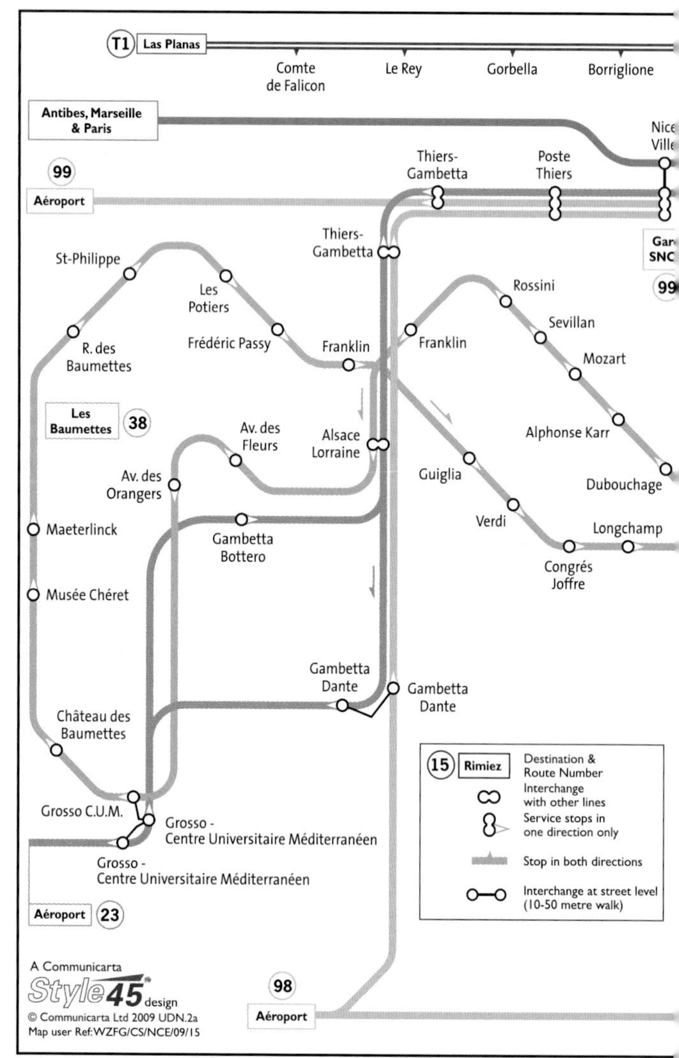

T1
Las Planas
Comte de Falicon
Le Rey
Gorbella
Borriglione
Antibes, Marseille & Paris
99
Aéroport
Thiers-Gambetta
Poste Thiers
St-Philippe
Les Potiers
R. des Baumettes
Frédéric Passy
Franklin
Rossini
Sevillan
Mozart
Les Baumettes
38
Av. des Fleurs
Alsace Lorraine
Alphonse Karr
Guiglia
Dubouchage
Av. des Orangers
Maeterlinck
Gambetta Bottero
Verdi
Longchamp
Congrés Joffre
Musée Chéret
Gambetta Dante
Château des Baumettes
Grosso C.U.M.
Grosso - Centre Universitaire Méditerranéen
Aéroport
23
15
Rimiez
Destination & Route Number
Interchange with other lines
Service stops in one direction only
Stop in both directions
Interchange at street level (10-50 metre walk)
A Communicarta Style45 design
© Communicarta Ltd 2009 UDN.2a
Map user Ref:WZFG/CS/NCE/09/15
98
Aéroport

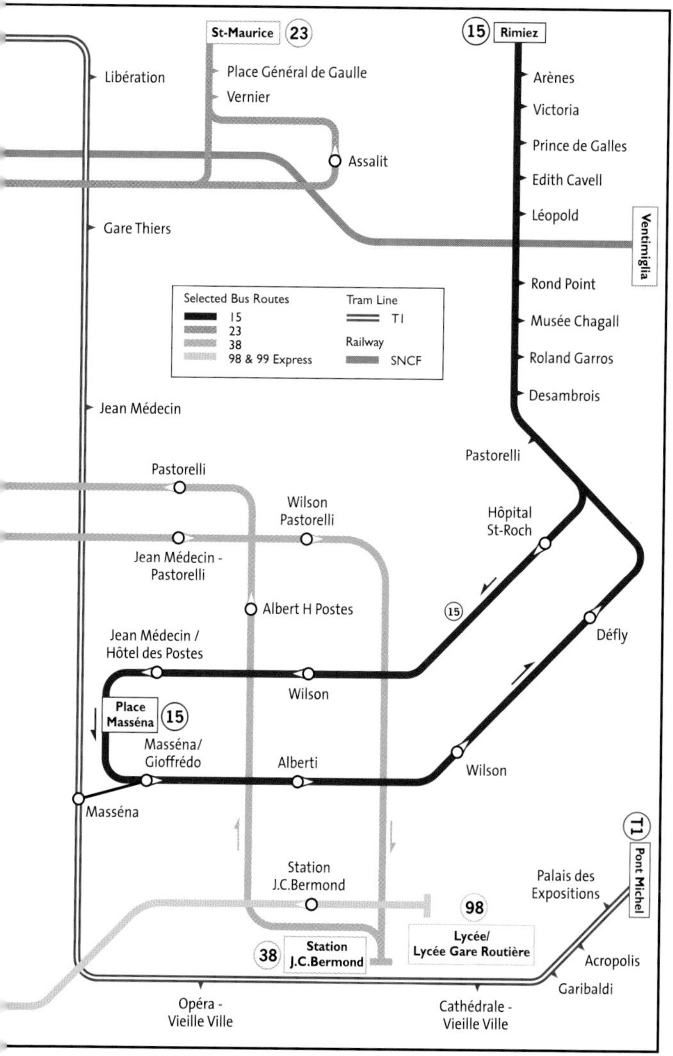

St-Maurice 23

15 Rimiez

Libération

Place Général de Gaulle

Vernier

Assalit

Arènes

Victoria

Prince de Galles

Edith Cavell

Léopold

Ventimiglia

Gare Thiers

Rond Point

Musée Chagall

Roland Garros

Desambrois

Selected Bus Routes
- 15
- 23
- 38
- 98 & 99 Express

Tram Line
- T1

Railway
- SNCF

Jean Médecin

Pastorelli

Pastorelli

Wilson Pastorelli

Hôpital St-Roch

Jean Médecin - Pastorelli

Albert H Postes

15

Défly

Jean Médecin / Hôtel des Postes

Wilson

Place Masséna 15

Masséna/ Gioffrédo

Alberti

Wilson

Masséna

T1 Pont Michel

Station J.C.Bermond

Palais des Expositions

98

Lycée/ Lycée Gare Routière

38 Station J.C.Bermond

Acropolis

Garibaldi

Opéra - Vieille Ville

Cathédrale - Vieille Ville

ORIENTATION

The centre of Nice is defined by the west-to-east seafront (promenade des Anglais, becoming the quai des Etats-Unis further east), the north–south avenue Jean Médecin, and the wide boulevard-flanked spaces of the Paillon (Nice's river, now covered over with parks and squares in the centre) coming down from the northeast and meeting Jean Médecin at place Masséna before continuing to the Jardin Albert 1er and promenade des Anglais. The west–east top of the walkable centre is formed by boulevard Victor Hugo, crossing Jean Médecin to become boulevard Dubouchage. The Italianate Old Town (Vieille Ville, also called Vieux Nice) is a triangular pocket of narrow streets and alleyways formed by the Paillon and the seafront, its third side being the green bulk of the Château hill. On the other side of the Château is the Port area. Between Jean Médecin, Victor Hugo and the promenade is the other main area of hotels, shops and restaurants, at its heart the pedestrian zone of rue de France and rue Masséna.

GETTING AROUND

It's no hardship to get around on foot in Nice – the entire length and breadth of the centre is no more than a 30–40-minute walk in any direction. For sights outside this area, you'll need to catch a bus or train.

Nice has an excellent bus system, day and night (night buses are called Noctambus), run by the regional company **Ligne d'Azur** (W www.lignedazur.com). A detailed bus map, which covers the city and most of the outlying places mentioned in this book, is obtainable from the tourist offices, but not, strangely, from the central bus station. All bus stops display their names, clear maps and timetables for the routes that serve them. The company also allows you to download a timetable for each of its routes from its website, which is worth

TOURS

A good way of seeing a lot of Nice in a short time is to take a tour. **Le Grand Tour** (04 92 29 17 00 09.30–18.50) is a hop-on, hop-off bus tour which takes in Cimiez to the north and Mont Boron in the east as well as the usual attractions. The full tour lasts 1½ hours if you don't get off, and fares for a one-day pass are around €20. You can book tickets at the tourist office or buy onboard. The **Petit Train Touristique** (www.petittrainnice.com) is a cheaper 40-minute tour, with commentary, of the Old Town and the Château hill. It operates every 30 minutes from 10.00–19.00 during summer, with shorter hours in spring and autumn and no service at all between November and January.

doing if you have particular destinations in mind, as the help desk at the central bus station is not very generous with them.

A single journey anywhere in Nice (or along the Côte d'Azur) costs €1, payable to the driver on boarding. He can also sell you a one-day pass (€4 for unlimited travel by one person in one day), a seven-day pass (€15 for unlimited travel by one person over seven consecutive days) or a Multi+ ticket (€20, which is good for 20 journeys and can be used by one or more people simultaneously).

After close to four years of chaotic construction, Nice's new tramway opened at the end of 2007. The line runs from Las Planas, in the northwest of the city, to Pont Michel in the northeast, passing Nice-Ville train station, avenue Jean-Médecin, the *gare routière* (bus station) and the Old Town along the way. There are machines to purchase tickets at each stop; these same tickets are also used on

Nice's buses. Be sure to pop your ticket into one of the validating machines when you get on the tram.

Local trains aren't much use to visitors for getting around within the city, but they are a great way to travel along the coast and into the mountains (see page 108). If you're planning on visiting various locations on the same day, the €12 Carte Isabelle (available from Nice-Ville railway station from 1 June to 30 September only) gives one day of unlimited travel on the regular trains between Cannes and the Italian border. For information on local trains, see ⓦ www.ter-sncf.com.

Taxis are not a cheap option in Nice, especially at night (19.00–07.00), when the rates are higher. You can pick up a cab from ranks in front of the Negresco, on promenade des Anglais, avenue Félix Faure, rue de l'Hôtel des Postes (at the back of Galeries Lafayette) or the main railway station. Otherwise call **Allo Taxi Riviera** (ⓣ 04 93 13 78 78 ⓛ 24 hrs).

The public car park underneath the flower market and Parking Infernet on the Port are centrally located options. The website ⓦ www.interparking-france.com also lists further information about car parks in Nice. On-street parking is hard to find, but even if you do you can expect other drivers to park so close that you can't get away when you want to.

CAR HIRE

All of the major rental companies and many local ones have offices around the main railway station, Gare Nice-Ville. A comprehensive list of locations is available on the tourist office website. Many hotels can arrange car hire, and usually have the car brought to the hotel.

The Vieille Ville looks more Italian in places than French

THE CITY OF
Nice

Old Nice & the Port

The Château hill and the Port below it was the site of the ancient Greek settlement Nikaia. Later, the medieval town grew up to the west in the triangle now known as the Vieille Ville (Old Town) or Vieux Nice. This is a partly pedestrianised maze of narrow streets opening out onto small squares, whose centre is the busy open space of cours Saleya, which adjoins the seafront of quai des Etats-Unis at the old fish market buildings. Apart from one or two municipal buildings, the look and feel of its colourful architecture is pure Italy, with a dash of North African souk at the northeast end. Many listings in this section are located in the pedestrianised zone and are therefore not reachable by public transport. To reach the edge of the pedestrianised zone, take the tram to stops Opéra-Vieille Ville or Cathédrale-Vieille Ville, or the bus to the gare routière (central bus station).

SIGHTS & ATTRACTIONS

Cathédrale de Ste-Réparate

North of rue de la Poissonnerie the Old Town becomes a warren of crowded but traffic-free alleys and streets. Follow the signs to 'Cathédrale' and you'll arrive in place Rossetti, a lively mass of café

WHAT'S IN A NAME?

You will notice that, in deference to Nice's unique local identity, most of the street names in the Vieille Ville are displayed in both French and the local dialect Niçard or Nissart, a dying language, which is currently kept alive by Nice's older generations.

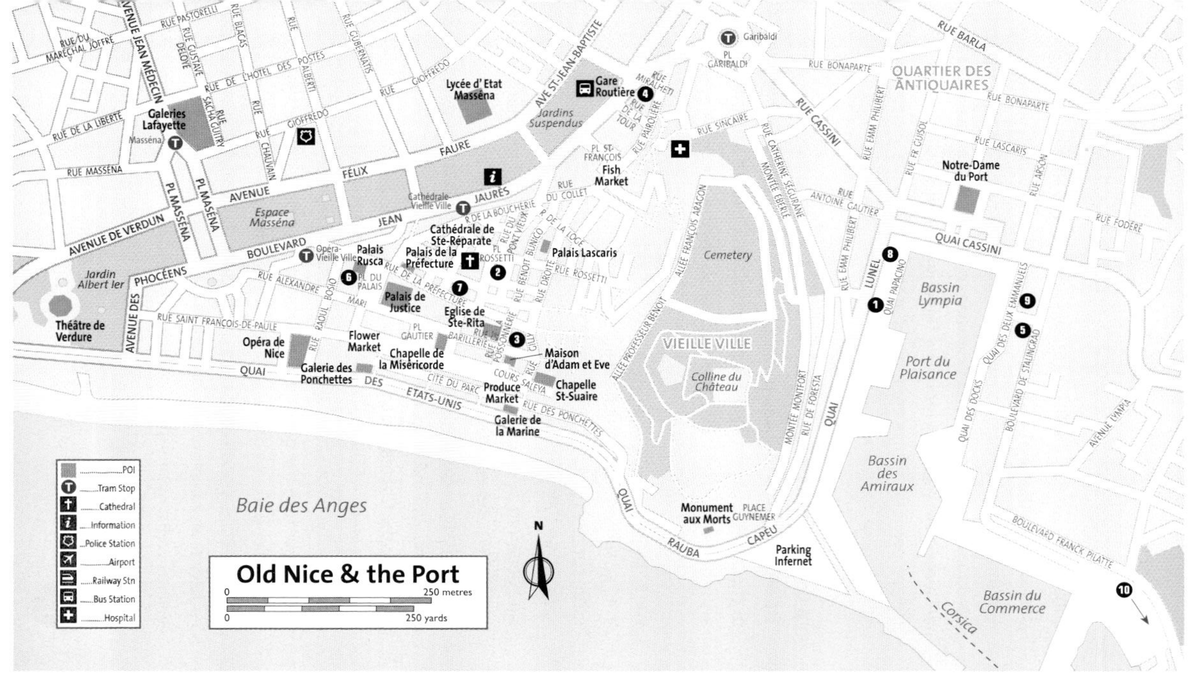
Old Nice & the Port
0
250 metres
0
250 yards
POI
Tram Stop
Cathedral
Information
Police Station
Airport
Railway Stn
Bus Station
Hospital
N
Baie des Anges
Galeries Lafayette
Lycée d' Etat Masséna
Gare Routière
Jardins Suspendus
Espace Masséna
Jardin Albert Ier
Théâtre de Verdure
Opéra de Nice
Galerie des Ponchettes
Flower Market
Chapelle de la Miséricorde
Palais Rusca
Palais de Justice
Palais de la Préfecture
Cathédrale de Ste-Réparate
Eglise de Ste-Rita
Palais Lascaris
Fish Market
Maison d'Adam et Eve
Produce Market
Chapelle St-Suaire
Galerie de la Marine
Cemetery
VIEILLE VILLE
Colline du Château
Monument aux Morts
Parking Infernet
QUARTIER DES ANTIQUAIRES
Notre-Dame du Port
Bassin Lympia
Port du Plaisance
Bassin des Amiraux
Bassin du Commerce
Corsica
Garibaldi
Masséna
Cathédrale-Vieille Ville
Opéra-Vieille Ville
AVENUE JEAN MÉDECIN
RUE PASTORELLI
RUE GUSTAVE DELOYE
RUE BLACAS
RUE GUBERNATIS
RUE DE L'HOTEL DES POSTES
RUE ALBERTI
RUE GIOFFREDO
RUE CHAUVAIN
RUE SACHA GUITRY
RUE DU MARECHAL JOFFRE
RUE DE LA LIBERTÉ
RUE MASSÉNA
PL MASSÉNA
AVENUE DE VERDUN
AVENUE FÉLIX FAURE
BOULEVARD JEAN JAURÈS
AVE ST-JEAN-BAPTISTE
AVENUE DES PHOCÉENS
RUE ALEXANDRE MARI
RUE RAOUL BOSIO
RUE SAINT FRANÇOIS-DE-PAULE
QUAI DES ETATS-UNIS
PL DU PALAIS
RUE DE LA PRÉFECTURE
PL GAUTIER
RUE BARILLERIE
CITÉ DU PARC
COURS SALEYA
RUE DE LA POISSONNERIE
RUE GILLY
RUE DES PONCHETTES
PL ROSSETTI
RUE ROSSETTI
R DE LA BOUCHERIE
RUE DU PONT VIEUX
RUE BENOIT BUNICO
R DE LA LOGE
RUE DROITE
RUE DU COLLET
PL ST-FRANÇOIS
RUE DE LA TOUR
RUE PAIROLIÈRE
RUE MIRALHETI
RUE SINCAIRE
PL GARIBALDI
RUE CASSINI
RUE CATHERINE SÉGURANE
MONTÉE EBERLÉ
ALLÉE FRANÇOIS ARAGON
ALLÉE PROFESSEUR BENOIT
MONTÉE MONTFORT
RUE DE FORESTA
QUAI LUNEL
QUAI RAUBA CAPEU
PLACE GUYNEMER
RUE EMM PHILIBERT
RUE ANTOINE GAUTIER
RUE BONAPARTE
RUE FR GUISOL
RUE LASCARIS
RUE ARSON
RUE FODÉRÉ
RUE BARLA
QUAI CASSINI
QUAI PAPACINO
QUAI DES DEUX EMMANUELS
QUAI DES DOCKS
BOULEVARD DE STALINGRAD
AVENUE LYMPIA
BOULEVARD FRANCK PILATTE

tables surrounding an 18th-century fountain, and Nice's cathedral, dedicated to the third-century Palestinian martyr Saint Réparate. The ornate plasterwork and bright colours, inside and out, are the baroque style at its most Mediterranean; Ste-Réparate was built between 1650 and 1757, replacing the original hilltop cathedral (see below). Don't miss the interior or the polychrome-tiled roof of the dome. ⓐ pl. Rossetti ◷ 07.30–12.00, 14.00–18.00

La Colline du Château

This commanding hill and public park was once the centre of power of the ancient Greek city of Nikaia and of the Dukes of Savoy, and was also the site of Nice's first cathedral of Ste-Marie, the ruins of which can still be seen at the top of the hill. The Château's fortifications were strong enough to withstand a combined Franco-Turkish siege in 1543; subsequent French assaults in 1691 and again in 1705 were more successful, and in 1706 Louis XIV ordered the demolition of the castle from which the hill takes its name. From 1783 the northern side began to be used as a burial ground – Catholic, Protestant and Jewish cemeteries still occupy this area – but in 1821 the city council had the happy idea of creating a public park, the Parc du Château, which was laid out in its present form after 1860.

Today the Château is a great place for strolling and taking in stunning views of the Old Town, the Port and the sea. If you are the energetic type you can walk the steps leading from the end of rue Rossetti, or take the easy way and use the *ascenseur* (lift) at the seafront end (€0.80 one way, €1.10 return). Atop the hill are several kilometres of easy walking paths, leading you to the ruins of the medieval cathedral, an orientation table and a cooling cascade facing the Vieille Ville, as well as a café and a children's playground. Note the interesting modern mosaics in pavements and steps on the eastern side. It's an

The narrow streets of the Vieille Ville all seem to lead to the cathedral

easy walk down, either back to the Old Town or to the Port.

Parc du Château 09.00–20.00 June–Aug; 09.00–19.00 Apr, May & Sept; 10.00–17.30 Oct–Mar

Château lift End of the quai des Etats-Unis, near the Hôtel Suisse 04 93 85 62 33 08.00–20.00 July & Aug; 08.00–19.00 May, June & Sept; 08.00–18.00 Oct–Apr

Cours Saleya

Rue St-François-de-Paule opens into this pedestrian area, the heart of the Old Town, which is thronged by visitors day and night. The colourful flower and produce market is held every day except Monday (produce during the morning only), accompanied by local craft stalls. Every square inch is reclaimed for restaurant tables as soon as the market departs. On Mondays the flowers give way to *brocante*, that useful French word covering everything from genuine antiques to junk. Two churches overlook cours Saleya: the Chapelle de la Miséricorde of 1740, with a magnificent baroque interior, and at the very end, on the corner of rue Gilly, the gold-coloured façade of the Chapelle St-Suaire, built for the use of the 17th-century judicial body, the Sénat.

Palaces

Midway along, cours Saleya opens out onto place Gautier, whose backdrop is the white Palais de la Préfecture, formerly the Palace of the Dukes of Savoy, built in the 17th century for use by the city's Italian rulers and now the seat of the Prefect of the Alpes-Maritimes *département*. Further along rue Alexandre Mari from the Préfecture is the neo-classical Palais de Justice (law courts), dominating the wide place du Palais, where every doorway is adorned with lawyers' brass plaques. Across the square is the Palais Rusca, with its jolly pink clock tower.

The east side of the Colline du Château overlooks the Port and Mont Boron

The Port

Nice's port is home to some luxurious yachts in the marina (Port du Plaisance and Bassin Lympia), from where you can also take day trips by boat to destinations such as Monaco, St-Tropez and the Ile Ste-Marguerite. A free shuttle bus will take you from any part of the quayside to the commercial port, which serves the giant car ferries to Corsica and Sardinia as well as the many Mediterranean cruise ships that call at Nice. The atmosphere of the Port de Plaisance is laid-back by day and night; the quaysides are where you'll find some of the best bars and seafood restaurants in Nice. From here it's an easy stroll back around the foot of the Château hill, passing Place Guynemer, along the quai Rauba Capéu and onto the main seafront of the quai des Etats-Unis. Bus: 1, 2, 7, 9, 10, 14, 81, 100

Rue Droite & Palais Lascaris

One of the most direct paths through the Old Town, rue Droite (or 'straight road') comes out at place St-François, where you'll see the old town hall and on Monday to Saturday mornings the tiny but lively fish market. En route you'll come across the **Palais Lascaris** (15 rue Droite 04 93 62 72 40 10.00–18.00 Wed–Mon), a perfectly preserved aristocratic town house, which appears as little more than a doorway onto the street. Enter and discover the monumental staircase and upstairs state rooms which often house art exhibitions. Highlights are the decorated ceilings of the entrance hall, the recreated apothecary's shop just inside the door and the first-floor chapel, used for noble family weddings. The top floor of the Palais houses the Musée de la Musique de Nice, dedicated to Niçois music, manuscripts and instruments, from the traditional to contemporary.

Aerial view of the Port de Plaisance

Rue de la Poissonnerie

On the corner of this narrow street, heading north from the eastern end of cours Saleya, you can see the last remaining decorated house in the Vieille Ville, the Maison d'Adam et Eve, dating from the 16th century. Tucked away on the opposite side a little further up is the 17th-century Eglise de Ste-Rita (also known as the Chapelle de l'Annonciation), dedicated to the patron saint of hopeless cases; the restored interior is a baroque jewel.

Rue St-François-de-Paule

Enter the Vieille Ville from the Jardin Albert 1er along this shop-lined street, which takes its name from the 18th-century church of St Francis of Paola (a popular French–Italian Renaissance friar, now officially the patron saint of Italian fishermen) on the left. Almost opposite is the city's Opéra, an imposing 1885 imitation of Garnier's Paris opera house.

CULTURE

If you want a complete change from the Vieille Ville's stunning array of baroque churches, head for the seafront and check out the changing exhibitions of contemporary artists' work at the Galerie des Ponchettes and Galerie de la Marine. Alternatively, head down the Old Town's rue Droite, where galleries compete for attention with eccentric paintings, unusual sculpture and a wide range of crafts.

Galerie de la Marine ⓐ 59 quai des Etats-Unis ⓣ 04 93 62 37 11 ⓛ 10.00–18.00 Tues–Sun

Galerie des Ponchettes ⓐ 77 quai des Etats-Unis ⓣ 04 93 62 31 24 ⓛ 10.00–18.00 Tues–Sun

RETAIL THERAPY

Aside from the flower and produce markets, from spring through autumn cours Saleya has a colourful night market of gifts, crafts, toys and the like, which range from the desirable to the weird. On Mondays (08.00–18.00) the bric-a-brac market is worth browsing for antiques, militaria, craft items and old cast-offs. If you see something you really like and you've got the time, it's worth bargaining. Place du Palais hosts specialist markets on Saturdays between 08.00 and 18.00: second-hand books (1st & 3rd Sats); paintings and crafts (2nd Sat); old postcards (4th Sat).

The Vieille Ville itself is packed with shops, high-quality specialist boutiques mingling with mass-market outlets.

L'Atelier des Cigales With gorgeous items literally spilling out onto the street, this is the place to go for candles, knick-knacks and the finest and funkiest in hand-painted tableware. ⓐ 13 rue du Collet ⓣ 04 93 85 70 62 10.30–19.30

L'Atelier des Jouets Follow the constant stream of bubbles to this corner shop, toys (many of them handmade) of the highest quality. ⓐ 7 rue Gilly ⓣ 04 93 13 09 60 10.30–19.00 Thur–Tues, 15.30–19.00 Wed

Oliviera For locally produced olive oil, head to Oliviera. Can't decide which type you'd like to take home? Stop for lunch or dinner, and a chance to taste owner Nadim's favourites, married with traditional Niçois dishes. ⓐ 2 rue Benoit Bunico ⓣ 04 93 13 06 45 ⓦ www.oliviera.com 10.00–23.00 Tues–Sat, 10.00–15.00 Mon & Sun

GOING CHEAP
The government strictly regulates Nice's twice-yearly sales periods, which usually occur around the beginning of January and the beginning of July. Hit the high-street shops around avenue Jean Médecin for some of the best bargains.

Poterie Painting encourages you to create a truly unique souvenir by designing and painting your own pottery; your (or your children's) artistic efforts are then glazed and fired ready to take away. ⓐ 1 rue du Pont Vieux ⓣ 04 93 80 51 77 ⓛ 10.00–18.00 Wed–Sat, 14.00–18.00 Sun

Quartier des Antiquaires is the place for real antique shops; in particular, the Village Ségurane, on the corner of rue Catherine Ségurane and rue Gautier, is a two-storey mall of quality antiques outlets. ⓐ Around rue Gautier, on the eastern side of the Château hill ⓦ Tram: Garibaldi

TAKING A BREAK

The choice of cafés for a quick coffee or drink or a light lunch is limitless. The liveliest areas are cours Saleya and place Rossetti, which has the added attraction of Fenocchio, an ice cream paradise. *Socca* (see page 30), baguettes and other take-away snacks are ubiquitous, with a definite North African/Middle Eastern bias to the fare on offer where rue Droite meets place St-François. There's no shortage of pizzerias in the Old Town for a quick lunch, but a one-course seafood meal at one of the restaurants lining the Port's quays can be surprisingly cheap.

Place Rossetti is a major hangout by day or night

Confiserie Florian £ ❶ Stop by at Florian to watch 30 years of confectionery techniques in action, then pop upstairs for a taste of your favourites. ⓐ 14 quai Papacino ⓣ 04 93 55 43 50 ⓦ www.confiserieflorian.com ◷ 09.00–12.00, 14.00–18.30 Bus: 1, 2, 7, 9, 10, 14, 81

Fenocchio £ ❷ This long-established ice cream parlour offers more flavours than you'd have thought possible – and every single one of them is fabulous. ⓐ 2 pl. Rossetti ⓣ 04 93 80 72 52 ⓦ www.fenocchio.fr ◷ 09.00–00.00

La Fougasserie £ ❸ Head to this excellent Old Town *boulangerie* and take your pick of their tasty quiches – carrot, tuna and tomato or spinach and *chèvre* (goat's cheese) are just some of the choices on offer. ⓐ 5 rue de la Poissonerie ⓣ 04 93 80 92 45 ◷ 08.00–19.30 Wed–Mon, Dec–Oct

René Socca £ ❹ The classic place for *socca*. Order food at the bar and your drinks at one of the outside tables, then wait for the food to be served. ⓐ 2 rue Miralheti ⓣ 04 93 92 05 73 ◷ 09.00–21.00 Tues–Sun

AFTER DARK

RESTAURANTS

Tartane £ ❺ Entirely off the beaten track, the Tartane is a home-style eatery with all the right stuff – the friendliest owners, the most fabulous pizza and giant jugs of chilled wine. All this, and at budget prices. ⓐ 44 blvd de Stalingrad ⓣ 04 93 89 66 91 ◷ 12.00–14.30, 19.30–22.30

La Merenda ££ ❻ This tiny restaurant serving French cuisine may offer little in the way of ambience, but for true foodies, a stop at Le Merenda is essential. ⓐ 4 rue Raoul Bosio (marked on some maps with the street's former name, rue de la Terrasse) ⓣ No reservations ⓛ 12.15–14.30, 19.00–22.00 Mon–Fri

Tire-Bouchon ££ ❼ As a change from Italian and *Nissard* dishes, sample the classic Lyonnais cuisine of this small restaurant just north of cours Saleya (booking advisable). ⓐ 19 rue de la Préfecture ⓣ 04 93 92 63 64 ⓦ www.le-tire-bouchon.com ⓛ 19.00–22.30

La Zucca Magica ££ ❽ 'The Magic Pumpkin' offers an entirely vegetarian, scrumptious five-course set menu. ⓐ 4 bis quai Papacino ⓣ 04 93 56 25 27 ⓦ www.lazuccamagica.com ⓛ 12.30–14.30, 19.30–22.30 Tues–Sat Tram: Garibaldi

L'Ane Rouge £££ ❾ 'The Red Donkey' is a long-established Michelin-starred restaurant on the eastern quay of the Port: fine dining, leaning

Nice harbour by night

to seafood and local specialities, at the sort of prices you'd expect. Booking advisable. ⓐ 7 quai des Deux Emmanuels ⓣ 04 93 89 49 63 ⓦ www.anerougenice.com ⓛ 12.00–14.00, 19.00–22.00 Fri–Tues, 19.00–22.00 Thur ⓝ Bus: 1, 2, 7, 9, 10, 14, 81, 100

Le Bistrot de la Réserve de Nice £££ ⑩ Chef Sébastien Mahuet serves up an ever-changing menu of seasonal specialities, with a side of sea views to die for. ⓐ Palais de la Réserve, 60 blvd Franck Pilatte ⓣ 04 97 08 14 80 ⓦ www.lareservedenice.com ⓛ 12.00–14.30, 19.00–22.30 ⓝ Bus: 20, 30

ENTERTAINMENT

Bar des Oiseaux A Nice institution, this bar/restaurant/theatre began life as a fictional creation in comedienne Noëlle Perna's radio show and she opened the real version in 1998. The live jazz adds to the atmosphere and there's also a 50-seat theatre putting on local productions (often in broad Niçois). ⓐ 5 rue st-Vincent, near place du Palais ⓣ 04 93 80 27 33 ⓦ www.bardesoiseaux.com ⓛ 12.00–14.00 Mon, 12.00–14.00, 19.30–23.00 Tues–Fri, 19.30–23.00 Sat

Ghost House A small and lively disco and bar whose DJs spin jazz, house and hip-hop. ⓐ 3 rue Barillerie ⓣ 04 93 92 93 37 ⓦ www.leghost-pub.com ⓛ 21.30–02.30

Guest Head to the eastern side of the Port to dance with the swish crowds stepping off their yachts. ⓐ 5 quai Deux Emmanuel ⓣ 04 93 56 83 83 ⓦ http://leguest.com ⓛ 23.00–05.00 ⓝ Bus: 1, 2, 7, 9, 10, 14, 81, 100

Opéra de Nice A full programme of concerts, ballet, recitals and opera, September to June. ⓐ 4–6 rue St-François-de-Paule ⓣ 04 92 17 40 00 ⓦ www.opera-nice.org

VIEWS & WALKS

Take an evening stroll from the pedestrianised place Garibaldi, down rue Cassini to the Port. The Port itself is magical at night, and one of the music bars around the harbour is likely to tempt you in for a drink or two. Continue along the quai Lunel and around the headland of the Château hill.

War memorials are not usually much of a tourist sight, but Nice's colossal Monument aux Morts (dedicated to the 4,000 Niçois who died during World War I) is a spectacular illuminated monument looking out to sea from the hillside. The views out to the Mediterranean from here are unforgettable, and as you round the quai Rauba Capéu you see the entire Baie des Anges magically defined by the lights of the seafront.

From mid-July to the end of August the city stages a 'promenade-spectacle', La Castellada (see below). Actors and musicians accompany an audience on a walk of the Château hill, stopping from time to time to portray the history of Nice, from the Ancient Greeks to the present day, through drama, comedy and music. You don't need a command of French to enjoy the spectacle.

La Castellada ⓐ Walks start from the lift to the Château (see page 64); Concerts in the old Château cathedral ⓣ 04 93 84 86 11 ⓒ 20.30 for a 21.00 start, Tues–Sat, mid July–end Aug. Admission charge; bookable through the tourist office

Western Nice

Most of the sights and activities of this district are confined to the busy area extending a few blocks west of avenue Jean Médecin and south of boulevard Victor Hugo down to the seafront. Wherever you wander in this section of Nice, don't forget to look up from time to time to enjoy the upper-storey architecture of the streets – all the wealth, frivolity and self-confidence of Nice's heyday is preserved in the wonderful façades of the villas and apartment blocks built in the late 19th century, culminating in the belle époque years before World War I. This is the area that rivals the Old Town in terms of the number of tourists – and the establishments that cater for them. At night, especially, the seafront acts as a magnet for locals and visitors alike, providing hours of free entertainment where the actors are also the audience. Further west and north are a few isolated attractions that are worth a journey out from the centre, including the unmissable Russian cathedral and several world-class museums.

SIGHTS & ATTRACTIONS

Cathédrale Orthodoxe Russe St-Nicolas (Russian Cathedral)

Well north of the centre of town, this has become Nice's most-visited single attraction, and remains the largest Russian Orthodox church outside the motherland. In a villa on this site in 1865 Grand Duke Nicholas, son and heir to the Russian Imperial throne, died at the age of 21. The aristocratic Russian expatriate community, led by the Czar and Czarina, had this basilica erected in his memory. It was completed in 1912, just before the Bolshevik Revolution swept away the society that built it, but was further enriched by ecclesiastical treasures that the fleeing nobility smuggled out of Russia. Today it is

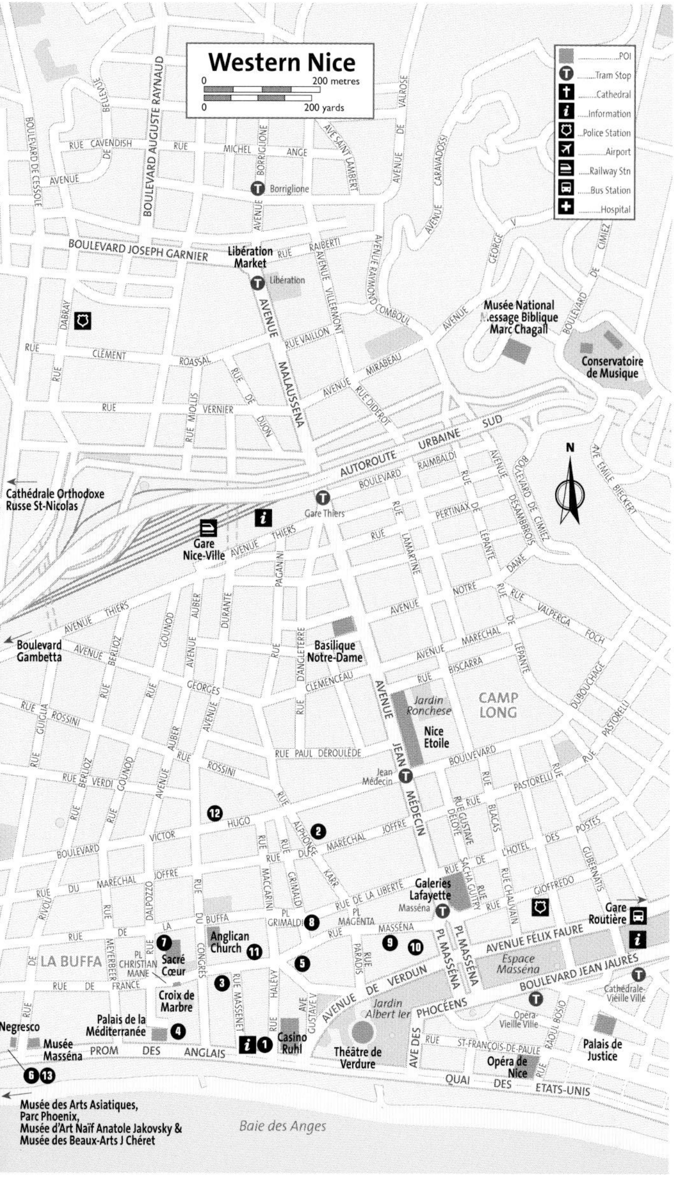
Western Nice
0 200 metres
0 200 yards
POI
Tram Stop
Cathedral
Information
Police Station
Airport
Railway Stn
Bus Station
Hospital
Borriglione
Libération Market
Libération
Musée National Message Biblique Marc Chagall
Conservatoire de Musique
Cathédrale Orthodoxe Russe St-Nicolas
Gare Thiers
Gare Nice-Ville
Boulevard Gambetta
Basilique Notre-Dame
Jardin Ronchese
Nice Etoile
CAMP LONG
Jean Médecin
Galeries Lafayette
Masséna
Gare Routière
LA BUFFA
Sacré Cœur
Anglican Church
Croix de Marbre
Palais de la Méditerranée
Negresco
Musée Masséna
Casino Ruhl
Théâtre de Verdure
Jardin Albert Ier
Espace Masséna
Opéra-Vieille Ville
Cathédrale-Vieille Ville
Palais de Justice
Opéra de Nice
PROM DES ANGLAIS
QUAI DES ETATS-UNIS
Musée des Arts Asiatiques, Parc Phoenix, Musée d'Art Naïf Anatole Jakovsky & Musée des Beaux-Arts J Chéret
Baie des Anges

The fairytale Russian cathedral

the mother church of Nice's new Russian community and its gilded onion domes guard a jewel box of icons and opulent frescoes. The self-guide sheets given to visitors explain the iconography in great detail and there is a nice selection of reproduction icons for sale in

the vestibule. As you walk along boulevard Tzarewitch to the cathedral from the bus stop, glance to your right to admire the art deco façade of the apartment block known as Le Palladium. ⓐ blvd du Tzarewitch, north of the main railway station ⓣ 04 93 96 88 02 ⓑ 09.00–12.00, 14.30–18.00 May–Sept; 09.15–12.00, 14.30–17.30 Oct & mid-Feb–Apr; 09.30–12.00, 14.30–17.00 Nov–mid-Feb ⓝ Bus: 4, 7 to Thiers-Gambetta; then walk under the motorway bridge to cross the road and turn left into boulevard Tzarewitch. Admission charge

Promenade des Anglais

The parasol-bedecked beaches, grand hotels and casinos of the promenade des Anglais, which takes its name from the wealthy British residents who built it for their seaside strolls in the early 19th century, typify the glamorous side of Nice. Today visitors from every country in the world stroll, rollerblade or jog along the world's most famous seaside prom, accompanied, it has to be said, by a ceaseless flow of traffic, while the wealthy patrons of hotels such as the Negresco and West End breakfast, lunch or sip cocktails on their glass-shielded terraces. The promenade connects with the central place Masséna via the avenue de Verdun, which along with the nearby rue de Paradis and avenue Gustave V is the favoured retail location of such upmarket icons as Cartier and Chanel. Between Verdun and avenue des Phocéens lies the park of the Jardin Albert 1er, which contains a jolly carousel for kids of all ages and the open-air Théâtre de Verdure, scene of the free *Musicalia* concerts (see page 20) and other events.

Marking the inner part of the promenade (which carries on west for several kilometres as far as the airport) stands the pink and white wedding cake of the Hôtel Negresco, the *grande dame* of Nice hotels since 1912 (see page 38). Like many old ladies, she is both stately and a little frivolous – how many hotels of her class would

feature a multicoloured plastic jazz musician (albeit created by French contemporary artist Niki de Saint-Phalle) outside their front door?

The imposing building opposite the Negresco is the Villa Masséna, the former home of a descendant of Marshal Masséna (see page 15). This houses the newly restored **Musée Masséna** (ⓐ 65 rue de France ⓣ 04 93 91 19 10 ⓛ 10.00–18.00 Wed–Sun). The museum's collection centres around the history of Nice, starting around the late 18th century. Of particular interest are photos, travel posters, menus and scale models from the early 20th century.

Further east along the promenade is the art deco façade of the Palais de la Méditerranée. What the Negresco was to the belle époque, the Palais became for the Jazz Age – the hotel of choice for millionaires, presidents and the stars. Built by the Dalmas brothers for American millionaire Frank Gould in 1930, it was the wonder of the age, with a 1,000-seater theatre and a casino. By 1978 it was derelict; the state declared the façade a national monument, but the remainder was demolished. Now a new grand hotel and casino sit, rather uncomfortably, behind Gould's masterpiece. Two blocks along, Nice's other casino, the Casino Ruhl, occupies the ground floor of the Meridien hotel. Bus: 11, 52, 59, 60, 62, 94, 98, 200, 400, 500, 710, 720

Rue de France & Rue Masséna

The side-streets leading up from the promenade are a mix of designer stores, nightclubs, grocery stores and fast-food outlets. Running along the top of them is rue de France, which is pedestrianised from the junction with rue du Congrès. Nearby, facing the little place Christine Mane, is one of the few historical monuments in this part of Nice, the Croix de Marbre, a marble cross erected in 1568 to celebrate a meeting between the three most powerful men in Europe

The art deco façade of the Palais de la Mediterranée hides a modern hotel

at the time: Pope Paul III, the Holy Roman Emperor Charles V and King François I of France. Opposite the Cross, a column commemorates visits by a later pope, Pius VII. In rue de la Buffa, just north of rue de France, is a little piece of England, the Anglican Church, built for the British expatriate community in 1862. The surrounding English cemetery dates from 1820. The remainder of rue de France, leading through rue Masséna to the very centre of the city at place Masséna, is a bustling pedestrianised thoroughfare with wall-to-wall restaurants, bars and shops, thronged with visitors and street entertainers. Busy but not too tacky, it has enough to keep the dedicated shopper or diner occupied for days.

CULTURE

Musée d'Art Naïf Anatole Jakovsky (Museum of Naive Art)
The Jakovsky Museum, one of Western Nice's trio of destination museums, opened in 1982 in the Château Sainte-Hélène, the former residence of the parfumier François Coty. It contains around 600 paintings, drawings, engravings and sculptures that chart the world of naive art from the 18th century to the present, including works by Bauchant, Bombois, Rimbert and Séraphine, and Croatian, Haitian and Brazilian artists. Ⓐ Château Ste Hélène, av. de Fabron Ⓣ 04 93 71 78 33 Ⓒ 10.00–18.00 Wed–Mon Ⓝ Bus: 9, 10, 11, 12, 23, 34

Musée des Arts Asiatiques (Oriental Art Museum) & Parc Phoenix
This 1998 minimalist building, designed by Japanese architect Kenzo Tange to embody Asian philosophical principles, is a work of art in its own right. The museum comprises a series of individual galleries, each devoted to a different Eastern civilisation, from China and Japan to Cambodia and India. There is also a Japanese tea room, where you can experience an authentic tea ceremony, and a multimedia centre for further study of Asiatic culture. The museum stands in the grounds of Parc Phoenix, which has 7 hectares (17 acres) of floral displays laid out on an ecological theme, exotic animals, plus the world's largest glasshouse, featuring tropical plants. The park puts on a varied programme of exhibitions; for details visit Ⓦ www.nice.fr and follow links under 'Nice Environnement'. Although these two attractions are a bus journey to the edge of town, they're well worth the trip. **Musée des Arts Asiatiques** Ⓐ 405 prom. des Anglais, near the airport Ⓣ 04 92 29 37 00 Ⓦ www.arts-asiatiques.com Ⓒ 10.00–18.00 Wed–Mon, May–mid-Oct; 10.00–17.00 Wed–Mon, mid-Oct–Apr Ⓝ Bus: 9, 10, 23

Parc Phoenix ⓣ 04 92 29 77 00 ⓛ 09.30–19.30 Apr–Sept; 09.30–18.00 Oct–Mar. Admission charge

Musée des Beaux-Arts J Chéret (Fine Arts Museum)
This museum stands in the western suburb of Les Baumettes. The beautiful former private villa of a Russian princess, built in 1876, houses a fine collection of paintings, from 17th-century Italian works to 19th- and 20th-century Romantics and Impressionists, including Degas, Boudin, Dufy and Sisley, as well as sculptures by Rodin and others. It is particularly strong in pieces by Nice's native masters Carle Van Loo and Jules Chéret. ⓐ 33 av. des Baumettes ⓣ 04 92 15 28 28 ⓦ www.musee-beaux-arts-nice.org ⓛ 10.00–18.00 Tues–Sun ⓝ Bus: 3, 8, 9, 10, 12, 22, 23

RETAIL THERAPY

Fashion boutiques and shoe shops crowd the sides of the *zone piétonne*. None of them stand out as destination shops, but they all offer more individual and original items than the big stores.

Near the eastern end of rue Masséna, leading down from the small place Magenta, is rue Paradis, one of Nice's centres for international designer names, including MaxMara, Armani, Chanel and Sonia Rykiel. Pick up whimsical necklaces and funky jewellery by Niçois designers at **Les Néreides** (ⓐ 12 rue Paradis). More famous brand names – Cartier, Hermès, Lacoste, Louis Vuitton, Yves St-Laurent, to name but a few – can be found around the corner on avenue de Verdun and avenue de Suede.

TAKING A BREAK

Cafés, bars, pizzerias and ice cream parlours abound in the *zone piétonne* and surrounding streets. Unless otherwise indicated, most open early morning and only shut when the last customer has gone home.

Café de la Promenade £ ❶ This neon-lit Italian-style café and ice cream parlour is great for watching the endless procession of life along the seafront. ⓐ Corner of prom. des Anglais and rue Halévy ⓣ 04 93 76 09 04 ◷ 08.00–00.00 Ⓝ Bus: 11, 52, 59, 60, 62, 94, 98, 200, 400, 500, 710, 720

Karr ££ ❷ Stop here for a light lunch (the daily menu is always a bargain) or a glass of wine. The people-watching at a pavement table is unbeatable. ⓐ 10 rue Alphonse Karr ⓣ 04 93 81 18 31 ◷ 08.30–01.00 Mon–Fri, 15.00–01.00 Sat Ⓝ Tram: Jean Médecin

▼ *Small boutiques cluster in rue Masséna*

Liber'Tea ££ ❸ Surrounded by shops in the pedestrian zone, this is an ideal spot for a cup of tea or an early evening aperitif. ⓐ 9 bis rue de la Liberté ⓣ 04 93 87 17 57 ⓛ 08.00–23.00 Mon–Sat ⓝ Tram: Masséna

Pingala Bar ££ ❹ Grab a coffee or a cocktail at this Indian-inspired open-air bar, on the hotel's third floor. Best enjoyed at sunset. ⓐ Palais de la Méditerranée, 15 prom. des Anglais ⓣ 04 92 14 76 01 ⓛ 10.00–01.00 ⓝ Bus: 11, 52, 59, 60, 62, 94, 98, 200, 400, 500, 710, 720, 790

Le Quebec ££ ❺ For a more substantial midday pit-stop, a lot of experts rate the pizzas at this busy restaurant as the best in town, and the size of the place guarantees you won't have to wait long, if at all, for a table. Great atmosphere at night, too. ⓐ 43 rue Masséna ⓣ 04 93 87 84 21 ⓦ www.crescere.fr ⓛ 11.00–01.00 Mon–Sat ⓝ Bus: 3, 7, 8, 9, 10, 14, 22, 52, 59, 94 200, 400, 500, 710, 720, 790

La Rotonde £££ ❻ If you're smartly dressed and want to treat yourself, why not book a lunch table at the brasserie in the Negresco – it's nowhere near as expensive as the upmarket ambience might suggest, and you might spot some famous faces (see page 89).

AFTER DARK

RESTAURANTS

Every national cuisine imaginable is available around this area. If you head off the main thoroughfares into the quieter north–south cross streets you're bound to make your own discoveries and save a little off the bill.

Texas City £ ❼ 'French-Texan' owner Frank Charat lays on a satisfying array of Tex-Mex food and hamburgers, with the bonus of proper cocktails. ⓐ 10 rue Dalpozzo ⓣ 04 93 16 25 75 ⓦ www.texas-city-restaurant.com ◷ 12.00–14.00, 19.00–23.00 Mon-Sat, 19.00–23.00 Sun

Noori's £–££ ❽ Well-reviewed Indian restaurant just off the main pedestrianised zone. Mumbai cuisine, good service. ⓐ 1 pl. Grimaldi ⓣ 04 93 82 28 33 ⓦ www.nooris.com ◷ 12.00–14.30, 19.00–23.00 Bus: 3, 7, 8, 9, 10, 14, 22, 52, 59, 94

Boccaccio ££ ❾ If you're into seafood, come here for gourmet fish dishes and platters of *fruits de mer* served by serious bow-tied waiters. The paella is the best in Nice. Arrive early if you want to sit outside; inside the décor has a nautical theme. ⓐ 7 rue Masséna ⓣ 04 93 87 71 76 ⓦ www.boccaccio-nice.com ◷ 12.00–15.00, 18.00–00.00

Maison de Marie ££ ❿ This courtyard restaurant, an oasis of calm, is accessed from the busy rue Masséna just by Boccaccio (see above) but is a world away from the bustle of the pedestrian zone. Good Provençal cooking and friendly, attentive service. Booking advisable. ⓐ 5 rue Masséna ⓣ 04 93 82 15 93 ⓦ www.lamaisondemarie.com ◷ 12.00–14.00, 19.00–23.00

Restaurant Keisuke Matsushima (formerly Kei's Passion) ££ ⓫ Try Japanese chef Keisuke's innovative blend of French cuisine with Asian undertones. ⓐ 22 rue de France ⓣ 04 93 82 26 06 ⓦ www.keisukematsushima.com ◷ 12.00–14.30 Tues–Fri, 19.30–22.30 Mon–Sat

Restaurant Stéphane Viano ££ ⓬ Former chef at the reputable Don Camillo, Stéphane recently opened his own place, focusing on modern Niçois dishes and plates of artsy pasta. Spacious and chic, this spot is definitely to be saved for a special night out. ⓐ 26 blvd Victor Hugo ⓣ 04 93 82 48 63 ⓛ 12.00–14.00, 19.30–22.00 Mon–Sat ⓝ Bus: 3, 7, 8, 9, 10, 14, 22, 52, 59, 94, 200, 400, 500, 710, 720, 750

La Rotonde & Le Chantecler ££–£££ ⓭ The convivial atmosphere of Jean-Denis Rieubland's La Rotonde brasserie in the Hôtel Negresco includes an indoor fairground carousel, and the set menu is very reasonably priced. Booking advised. For more formal and expensive dining in opulent Regency surroundings, book for the Michelin-starred restaurant Le Chantecler – same location, same exceptional chef. ⓐ Hôtel Negresco, 37 prom. des Anglais ⓣ 04 93 16 64 00 ⓦ www.hotel-negresco-nice.com ⓛ La Rotonde: 07.00–23.00; Le Chantecler: 12.00–14.00, 19.30–22.00 Wed–Sun ⓝ Bus: 11, 52, 59, 60, 62, 94, 98, 200, 400, 500, 710, 720, 790 ⓘ Le Chantecler closed Jan-mid Feb

Book at Le Chantecler for a Michelin-starred, opulent dining experience

ENTERTAINMENT

The area just behind the promenade is the place to hunt out late-night clubs and bars with dancing; some also feature cabaret with showgirls. These streets can get a bit sleazy late at night, so don't leave a venue alone. Smart dress and a small entrance fee (and your passport, if you intend to gamble) will get you into the two big casinos on the promenade. A casino visit can be a complete night out – both have bars and restaurants that are a big attraction in themselves, and both put on special themed nights (Creole, Spanish, Tex-Mex evenings, and so on) in the summer season. For a separate admission charge you can watch a Vegas-style show and dance to a disco afterwards at the Ruhl, and the Palais stages cabaret and other performance events during the winter, and also hosts the Miss Nice contest.

Le Before Keep your eyes peeled for Le Before's unassuming doorway – this is one of the best places to enjoy cool cocktails and great DJs until the early hours of the morning. In warm months, get there

KNOW YOUR ROULETTE

For the uninitiated, French roulette is the kind where everybody crowds round the table, while the English version has a limited number of table seats, and the players all bet in chips of their own colour (so much more orderly). American roulette gives the bank two chances of taking everyone's money, with a zero and a double zero on the wheel.

HITTING THE PROMENADE

Everyone in Nice hits the promenade des Anglais at night at least once a week. The local youth take to their cars and motorbikes, while everybody else walks up and down. This is Nice's version of the Italian *passeggiata*, and the point is just to see and be seen and to take in the night-time views of the light-fringed bay. In the summer you may well be able to catch a free concert at the Théâtre de Verdure, but if not there will be plenty of home-grown talent – musicians and performers – on the seafront. The beach is popular during the day for impromptu picnics, volleyball games or just hanging out (but leave when the crowds start to thin out – it's not the safest place at night – and *never* be tempted to sleep out on it).

before 22.00 to enjoy happy hour (complete with snacks) on the terrace. ⓐ 18 rue du Congrès ⓣ 04 93 87 85 59 ⓑ 18.00–00.30 Mon–Sat ⓝ Bus: 217

Casino Ruhl 350 slot machines, plus blackjack, English and French roulette and poker tables. ⓐ 1 prom. des Anglais ⓣ 04 93 03 12 22 ⓦ www.lucienbarriere.com ⓑ 10.00–dawn ⓝ Bus: 11, 52, 59, 60, 62, 94, 98, 200, 400, 500, 710, 720, 790

Palais de la Méditerranée Blackjack, stud poker and American and French roulette tables. ⓐ 15 prom. des Anglais ⓣ 04 92 14 68 00 ⓦ www.lepalaisdelamediterranee.com ⓑ 10.00–dawn ⓝ Bus: 11, 52, 59, 60, 62, 94, 98, 200, 400, 500, 710, 720, 790

Eastern Nice

East of avenue Jean Médecin, Nice is a collection of disparate areas and suburbs, without any specific focus except for the 'green belt' of the Paillon (Nice's river, now covered in parks and squares). Walking eastwards from here leads to the area just north of the Port, which includes place Garibaldi and the Terra Amata Museum. Further east of the centre are the hillsides of Mont Alban and Mont Boron, which are good for a quick escape into the fresh air. Last but not least, the northern middle-class suburb of Cimiez has a clutch of cultural attractions that easily justify the bus journey.

SIGHTS & ATTRACTIONS

Cimiez

The quiet suburb of Cimiez, standing on what was the Roman settlement of Cemenelum, is home to a whole clutch of attractions, all next to one another. Tucked away in a quiet side-street at the southern tip of the suburb is one of Nice's must-see sights, the Musée National Message Biblique Marc Chagall. Further north lie the other major cultural draws, the Arènes, Museé Matisse and the Franciscan Monastery, all close together and served by the same bus stop. As you approach by bus you can't miss an enormous building with monogrammed windows; now an apartment block, this was once the hotel Excelsior Regina, where Queen Victoria stayed on her visits to Nice. It was also Matisse's home throughout much of the 1940s and 1950s. The Musée Matisse stands across the street in the grounds of the Arènes de Cimiez, the remains of the original 4,000-seater Roman amphitheatre (a small one by Roman standards). Today the arena still provides entertainment for the citizens, most

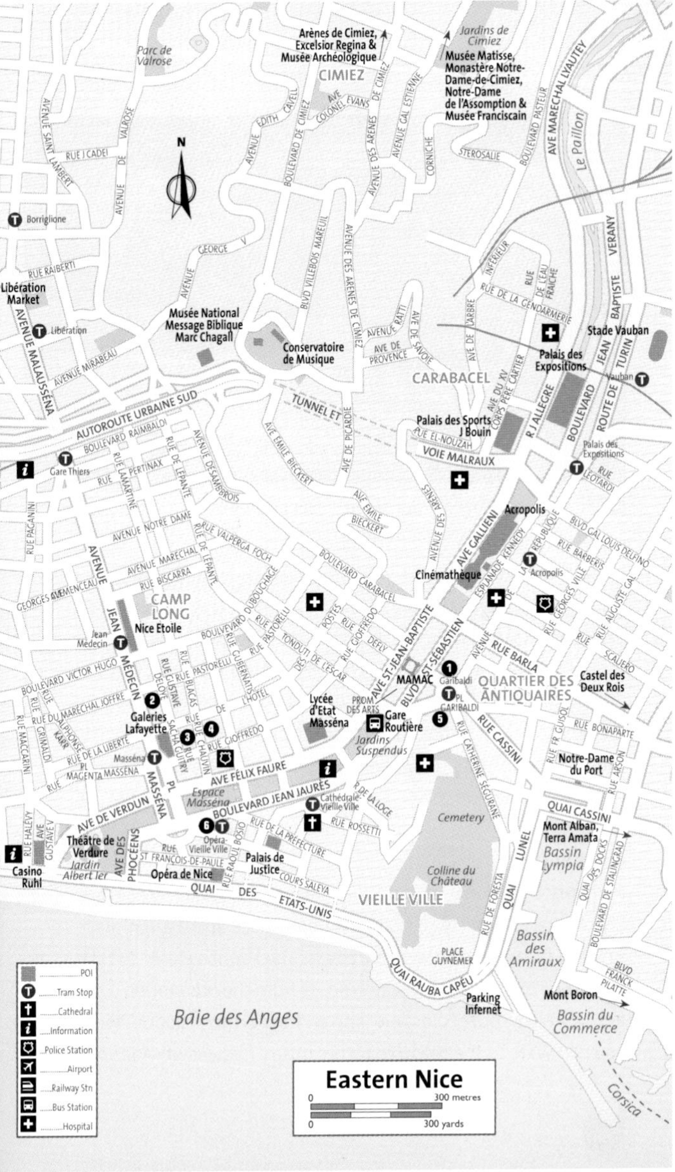
Eastern Nice
0
300 metres
0
300 yards
POI
Tram Stop
Cathedral
Information
Police Station
Airport
Railway Stn
Bus Station
Hospital
Arènes de Cimiez, Excelsior Regina & Musée Archéologique
Jardins de Cimiez
Musée Matisse, Monastère Notre-Dame-de-Cimiez, Notre-Dame de l'Assomption & Musée Franciscain
Parc de Valrose
CIMIEZ
Le Paillon
Borriglione
Libération Market
Libération
Musée National Message Biblique Marc Chagall
Conservatoire de Musique
Stade Vauban
Palais des Expositions
CARABACEL
Vauban
AUTOROUTE URBAINE SUD
TUNNEL ET
Gare Thiers
Palais des Sports J Bouin
VOIE MALRAUX
Palais des Expositions
Acropolis
Cinémathèque
Acropolis
CAMP LONG
Nice Etoile
Jean Médecin
MAMAC
Garibaldi
QUARTIER DES ANTIQUAIRES
Castel des Deux Rois
Galeries Lafayette
Lycée d'Etat Masséna
Gare Routière
Jardins Suspendus
Masséna
Notre-Dame du Port
Espace Masséna
Cathédrale-Vieille Ville
Cemetery
Théâtre de Verdure
Jardin Albert Ier
Opéra-Vieille Ville
Palais de Justice
Mont Alban, Terra Amata
Bassin Lympia
Casino Ruhl
Opéra de Nice
Colline du Château
VIEILLE VILLE
QUAI DES ETATS-UNIS
Bassin des Amiraux
PLACE GUYNEMER
QUAI RAUBA CAPEU
Parking Infernet
Mont Boron
Baie des Anges
Bassin du Commerce
Corsica
AVENUE MALAUSSÉNA
AVENUE JEAN MÉDECIN
BOULEVARD JEAN JAURÈS
AVE FÉLIX FAURE
AVE DE VERDUN
BOULEVARD CARABACEL
AVE GALLIENI
AVE ST-JEAN-BAPTISTE
BLVD ST-SÉBASTIEN
RUE CASSINI
QUAI CASSINI
QUAI LUNEL
RUE BARLA
BOULEVARD VICTOR HUGO
COURS SALEYA

The remains of Roman Nice at the Arènes de Cimiez

notably at the Jazz Festival. Nearby, the Musée Archéologique puts the visible remains of the Roman town in context. A short walk away is the Monastère Notre-Dame-de-Cimiez (the old Franciscan Monastery) and its associated church of Notre-Dame de l'Assomption. The monastery garden is a peaceful oasis of rose beds, next to a cemetery in which the artists Matisse and Dufy are buried. The monastery cloisters host open-air concerts in summer, and the Franciscan Museum is worth a visit. Bus: 15, 17

Mont Boron

In theory, if you keep walking eastwards you'll reach the commanding hill of Mont Boron, Nice's biggest open space and a great place to unwind from the bustle of the city. In practice, it's easier to take a bus from the city centre: if you catch no. 82 from the bus station you should get off at the Route Forestière stop on the northern slopes, from where you can walk to the massive 16th-century fortress of Mont Alban,

222 metres (728 ft) above sea level, affording exceptional panoramic views of the Riviera and Italy. Alternatively, take bus no. 14 from place Masséna all the way to its terminus on the summit of the Parc Forestier du Mont Boron. By walking down the footpaths towards the sea from here you will eventually find yourself back on a bus route, the no. 81, which will deposit you back at the *gare routière*. With its 142 pine-clad acres, 11 km (7 miles) of marked pathways and rare species of wild flowers, the forest of Mont Boron is a favourite haunt of joggers, botanists and walkers. There are magnificent views of St-Jean-Cap-Ferrat to the east and the Baie des Anges to the west.

North & east of the Port

Across boulevard St-Sébastien from MAMAC lies the pedestrianised place Garibaldi, an elegant 18th-century square, which was where Nice first expanded from the medieval confines of the Vieille Ville. The statue of Garibaldi, hero of Italian reunification, who was born in the city, looks on. Continuing along rue Cassini, past the Quartier des Antiquaires (see page 72), and ignoring the many signs for the Foreign Legion recruitment office, you arrive at the neoclassical church of Notre-Dame du Port, whose statue of the Virgin overlooks the bustle of the Bassin Lympia. Beyond the Port is the little hill of Castel des Deux Rois, with its children's amusement park and the prehistoric site of Terra Amata (see page 101).

Le Paillon

Place Masséna was pedestrianised in 2007 in preparation for the long-awaited tram system, and is now home to a gorgeous, gigantic fountain, located at the southern edge of the place. Leading east out of place Masséna is avenue Félix Faure, the northern flank of the continuous open space marking the old course of the river Paillon.

Espace Masséna is a large public square with fountains and greenery, looking across to the towers of the Old Town, which hosts local events and parades from time to time. Over the *gare routière*, the central bus station, is the rather grandly named terrace of the Jardins Suspendus or Hanging Gardens of the Paillon, which face the immense Lycée d'Etat Masséna, built in an exuberant style of decorated towers and cornices, a kind of Mediterranean Seaside Gothic.

Another hard-to-miss building is the vast grey monolith which houses MAMAC (see page 98) and the public library; further north still are the Acropolis conference centre, with the Cinémathèque (see below) and, at its far end, the Palais des Expositions trade fair hall.

CULTURE

Eastern Nice is rich in cultural attractions; even if you only visit a few of the museums and galleries listed below you will still experience some of the best of the city's masterpieces.

Cinémathèque de Nice

Founded in 1976 by Henri Langlois and dedicated to international film heritage, the Cinémathèque presents an ever-changing programme of classic films, on themes based around the work of a director or performer. It also works to preserve classic films and hosts conferences. To view the forthcoming programme, visit the website; to see a film you need only turn up, become a subscriber for a fee of €1, and then pay a modest €2 per film. ⓐ On the eastern side of the Acropolis centre, 3 espl. Kennedy ⓣ 04 92 04 06 66 ⓦ www.cinematheque-nice.com ⓛ Sept–July ⓝ Tram: Acropolis

◐ *The elegant Espace Masséna is a gateway to the Vieille Ville*

Musée Archéologique de Nice-Cimiez (Archaeological Museum of Nice)

The museum charts the history of civilisation in Nice and the Alpes-Maritimes region (of which Nice was the Roman capital). The collection includes well-preserved Roman baths dating back to the second and third centuries AD, as well as ceramics, glass, coins, jewellery, sculptures and tools ranging from the Bronze and Iron Ages to the Dark Ages. A small shop offers reproductions of some of the exhibits. ⓐ 160 av. des Arènes ⓣ 04 93 81 59 57 ⓦ www.musee-archeologique-nice.org ◷ 10.00–18.00 Wed–Mon ⓝ Bus: 15, 17

Musée d'Art Moderne et d'Art Contemporain – MAMAC (Modern Art Museum)

The permanent collection, dating from 1990, is dedicated to the related schools of French Nouveau Réaliste and American pop art, and pays particular attention to the Nice School of the last 30 years. There is a constantly changing programme of temporary exhibitions. Not only a must for all serious students of modern art, the pop art collection is fun for the casual visitor, too. ⓐ prom. des Arts ⓣ 04 93 62 42 01 ⓦ www.mamac-nice.org ◷ 10.00–18.00 Tues–Sun ⓝ Tram: Garibaldi

Musée Franciscain (Franciscan Museum)

Part of the Franciscan Monastery of Cimiez, this museum is devoted to St Francis of Assisi and the history of the order he founded, through paintings, sculptures, engravings, illuminated manuscripts, frescoes, and a reconstructed chapel and monk's cell. ⓐ pl. du Monastère ⓣ 04 93 81 00 04 ◷ 10.00–12.00, 15.00–18.00 ⓝ Bus: 17

The promenade des Arts' uncompromising architecture is hard to miss

Musée Matisse

Housed in and underneath a handsome red-painted 17th-century villa next to the Arènes de Cimiez, the original collection was donated by the artist himself in 1953. In addition to his paintings, drawings, engravings and sculptures, many of his favourite possessions are on display. Henri Matisse, who along with Raoul Dufy is the best-known artist of the Fauve school, lived in Nice from 1917 until his death in 1954. The works on show range from his earliest paintings of 1890 to his famous gouache cut-outs, and the museum holds a copy of every book he illustrated. There is also a well-stocked shop for prints and other souvenirs of Matisse and other French artists. ⓐ 164 av. des Arènes de Cimiez ⓣ 04 93 81 08 08 ⓦ www.musee-matisse-nice.org ⓛ 10.00–18.00 Wed–Mon ⓝ Bus: 15, 17

Musée National Message Biblique Marc Chagall (Chagall Museum of the Message of the Bible)

This museum is one of the cultural highlights of any stay in Nice. It was opened in 1972 through the efforts of Chagall himself, to house his enormous body of work on Biblical themes, consisting of paintings, sculptures, stained-glass windows, mosaics and tapestries, preparatory sketches, gouaches, engravings and lithographs. The 17 large canvases that are the highlight of the exhibition were painted between 1954 and 1967; Chagall's interpretations of the *Creation of Man* and *The Garden of Eden* are particularly stunning. There are also temporary exhibits of other themes to which he returned again and again, such as the circus. The building itself is the work of André Hermant, a follower

MARC CHAGALL

Born 1887 into a poor Orthodox Jewish family in Vitebsk, now in Belarus, Chagall spent his early career in St Petersburg and Paris, where he mixed with the Fauvists, Surrealists, Cubists and other avant-garde artists of the day. After a brief spell as an official artist in Bolshevik Russia, he wandered between Berlin, New York and Paris, developing a unique style in which brilliant colour and the frequent reappearance of a range of iconic characters are the most obvious elements. In 1949 Chagall settled in the Nice area, as had Matisse and Picasso, and he died in St-Paul-de-Vence at the age of 97. He mastered an astonishing range of media, from stained glass to lithography. A deeply religious man all his life, he was inspired by a visit to the Holy Land in 1930 to begin his Biblical masterpieces.

of Le Corbusier, and stands in a small garden. The on-site shop sells books and excellent reproductions of Chagall's works. ⓐ av. du Dr Ménard, corner of blvd de Cimiez ⓣ 04 93 53 87 20 ⓦ www.musee-chagall.fr ◷ 10.00–18.00 Wed–Mon, July–Sept; 10.00–17.00 Wed–Mon, Oct–June ⓝ Bus: 19, 22. Admission charge, free 1st Sun of the month

Musée de Paléontologie Humaine de Terra Amata (Museum of Human Prehistory)

Taking its name from the earliest inhabited site to be excavated here, this well-arranged museum is devoted to the seven-million-year history of humans, and specifically the last 900 millennia. The area around Nice is one of the longest-inhabited sites in Europe and rich in the remains of prehistoric man. The story that Terra Amata tells is fascinating anyway, but the local finds add a special relevance; it's not everywhere that possesses a 400,000-year-old camp of elephant-hunting *Homo erectus*, who predated *Homo sapiens* by over 350,000 years and seems to have developed communication skills. Ever-changing temporary exhibitions add to the experience and the museum shop is a good place for unusual souvenirs.
ⓐ 25 blvd Carnot ⓣ 04 93 55 59 93 ⓦ www.musee-terra-amata.org ◷ 10.00–18.00 Tues–Sun ⓝ Bus: 81, 100

RETAIL THERAPY

The east side of avenue Jean Médecin is dominated by the Galeries Lafayette department store on the corner of place Masséna, and two blocks north there's a day's worth of shopping at the multi-storey Etoile centre, with over 200 shops and specialist boutiques, including familiar names such as Habitat. The nearby branch of

FNAC sells books (including English-language), CDs and electronic and photographic products, and is the place to buy tickets for concerts and other events. The avenue is also a centre for bags and leather goods, with at least ten dedicated shops. Shops on the streets east of Jean Médecin tend to be for local, practical needs, but include some specialists.

Bruno Charvin Arts Everything a budding Renoir or Matisse could desire; you might not be able to get one of their massive easels onto the plane but there are plenty of other smaller artists' items that make good presents from the City of Art. ⓐ 39 rue Gioffredo ⓣ 04 93 92 92 82 ⓛ 10.00–19.00 Mon–Sat ⓡ Tram: Masséna

Go Sport The only large sports shop in central Nice, Go Sport is the place to pick up goggles, snorkels, a swimming costume or even roller-blades. ⓐ 13 place Masséna ⓣ 04 93 92 86 10 ⓦ www.go-sport.com ⓛ 10.00–19.30 Mon–Fri, 09.30–19.30 Sat ⓡ Tram: Masséna

Libération Market Join the locals and head north of the main train station to visit this massive bustling daily market. ⓐ av. Malausséna, place Général de Gaulle ⓛ 08.00–13.00 Tues–Sun ⓡ Tram : Libération

Résonances Stocking a soothing range of French organic soaps, after-sun products and bath oils. ⓐ 31 av. Notre Dame ⓣ 04 92 00 71 15 ⓦ www.resonances.fr ⓛ 10.00–19.00 Mon–Sat ⓡ Tram: Jean Médecin or Gare Thiers

---

If you're an artist rather than an art collector, head for Bruno Charvin

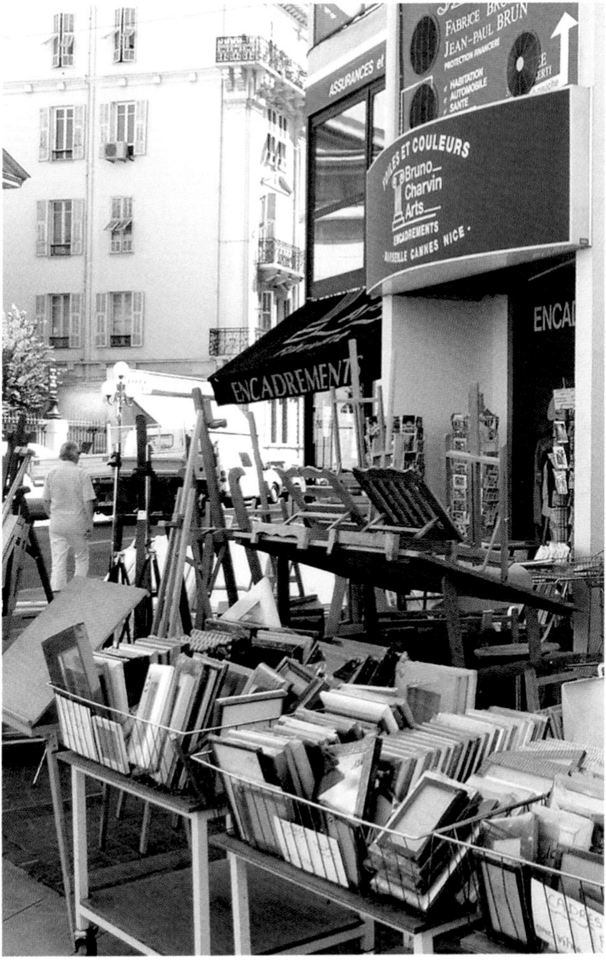
FABRICE BRUN
JEAN-PAUL BRUN
PROTECTION FINANCIERE
HABITATION
AUTOMOBILE
SANTE
ASSURANCES et
TOILES ET COULEURS
Bruno
Charvin
Arts
ENCADREMENTS
MARSEILLE CANNES NICE
ENCADREMENTS

Voyageurs du Monde Part travel agency, part bookstore with one of the best selections of travel guides and other useful tourism literature in Nice. Many books are in English. ⓐ 4 rue du Maréchal Joffre ⓣ 04 97 03 64 65 ⓦ www.vdm.com ⓛ 09.00–19.00 Mon–Sat ⓝ Tram: Jean Médecin

TAKING A BREAK

The air-conditioned coolness of the Etoile centre has a lot to recommend it for a coffee-break during shopping; there are two cafés in the atrium (bring your laptop and take advantage of the free WiFi hotspots) and more on each shopping floor. For more traditional outdoor cafés and bars, make for short but sweet rue Biscarra, behind Monoprix, or boulevard Jean Jaurès on the south side of the Paillon green space. If you're visiting the Terra Amata museum, the nearest cafés and lunch stops are in the Port area, where you'll be spoilt for choice. There's also a small café in the garden of the Chagall Museum, but nothing around the Arènes area. If you're planning a day out on Mont Boron, take a picnic.

AFTER DARK

RESTAURANTS

Au Petit Gari £–££ ❶ Friendly and very funny staff serve up traditional pan-French food in a bistro atmosphere. If you stop in for lunch, the amazing €13 set menu includes the dish of the day, a glass of wine and a coffee. ⓐ 2 pl. Garibaldi ⓣ 04 93 26 89 09 ⓦ www.aupetitgari.com ⓛ 12.00–14.00, 19.00–22.00 Mon–Fri ⓝ Tram: Garibaldi

Baie d'Amalfi ££ ❷ Satisfying and authentic Italian food and wine

in an elegant arcaded dining room decorated with views of the Neapolitan coast. Close to av. Jean Médecin. ⓐ 9 rue Gustave Deloye ⓣ 04 93 80 01 21 ⓦ www.baie-amalfi.com ⓛ 12.30–14.30 & 19.00–22.30 Tues-Sat, 12.30–15.00 Sun, Aug–June ⓣ Tram: Masséna

Brasserie Flo ££ ❸ A stone's throw from place Masséna, this brasserie, part of the same group that owns the legendary Bofinger and Boeuf sur le Toit in Paris, is a destination in its own right. Taking its cue from the original use of its building by the Folies-Bergères, Flo is set out as a theatre; the diners are the audience and the kitchen is actually on stage. The dishes are imaginative and very reasonably priced; there's even a special menu for late-night diners. ⓐ 4 rue Sacha Guitry ⓣ 04 93 13 38 38; ⓦ www.flonice.com ⓛ 12.00–14.30, 19.00–00.00 ⓣ Tram: Masséna

Caffè Bianco ££ ❹ It's easy to overlook this tiny restaurant, which is nestled between myriad shops. But what a mistake that would be! Enjoy modern French cuisine in the candlelit atmosphere – go early, as it tends to fill up very quickly. ⓐ 9 rue Chauvain ⓣ 04 93 13 45 12 ⓛ 12.00–14.30, 19.00–22.30 Tues–Fri, 19.00–22.30 Sat & Sun ⓣ Tram: Masséna

Grand Café de Turin ££ ❺ Not far from the edge of the Vieille Ville on a corner of one of Nice's liveliest squares, this seafood specialist has been famous for its *fruits de mer* for over a century. The décor is plain, the service a bit patchy at busy times, but you're unlikely to taste better shellfish in Nice. ⓐ 5 pl. Garibaldi ⓣ 04 93 62 29 52 ⓛ 08.00–23.00 ⓣ Tram: Garibaldi

L'Univers de Christian Plumail ££ ❻ Original and stylish cuisine from master chef Christian Plumail, at very affordable prices, especially if you order from the set menu, which is changed weekly. ⓐ 54 blvd Jean Jaurès ⓣ 04 93 62 32 22 ⓦ www.christian-plumail.com ⓛ 12.00–14.30 Tues–Fri, 19.45–22.30 Mon–Sat ⓝ Tram: Opéra-Vieille Ville

ENTERTAINMENT

Eastern Nice is not noted for its lively nightlife, but Cimiez hosts some important annual entertainments, including the following.

Les Concerts du Cloître This festival of chamber music follows on from the Jazz Festival at the end of July and extends into early August. Two weeks of night-time open-air performances in the cloisters of the Franciscan Monastery in Cimiez. ⓐ Opéra de Nice & Clôitre du Monastère de Cimiez ⓣ 08 00 95 08 50 ⓦ http://concerts.hexagone.net ⓛ late July–early Aug ⓝ Bus: 17

Nice Jazz Festival First staged in 1948, this international celebration of the French love affair with jazz features simultaneous performances on several stages, alongside stalls selling instruments, CDs, books and local food and drink. Over 500 musicians participate in 120 separate performances. Artists make for clubs, bars and hotels to continue after their official sessions. The atmosphere of this family-friendly event (with its own 'children's village' for 5- to 12-year-olds run by qualified supervisors) makes for a great evening. ⓐ Arènes et Jardins de Cimiez ⓣ 08 92 26 83 622 ⓦ www.nicejazzfestival.fr ⓛ 18.00–00.00 Sat–Sat over eight days in late July ⓝ Bus: 15, 17

◐ *St-Paul-de-Vence preserves its medieval atmosphere*

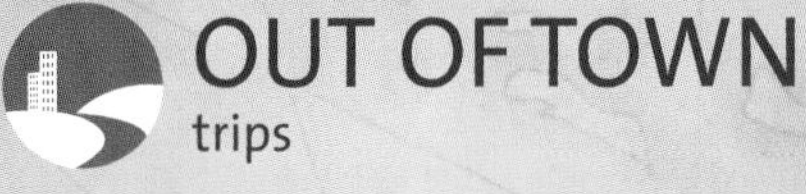

OUT OF TOWN trips

Seeing the Riviera

One of the great things about Nice is that it's so easy to leave it. Not that you're necessarily going to tire of the city quickly, but it is the best possible centre for visiting other parts of the Riviera, the mountainous backdrop of the Alpes-Maritimes and even Italy. The excursions in the following chapters are only a few of the days out that are possible using Nice's excellent transport connections.

TRIPS BY TRAIN

A cheap and comfortable way to get around, the excellent coastal rail service from the main railway station, Gare Nice-Ville (see page 51), puts you in touch with the rest of the coast, with literally dozens of trains per day. Buy tickets at the machines found at all railway stations on this route; they are easy to use, have instructions in English and give change. The following is a round-up of destinations and journey times.

Heading east: Villefranche-sur-Mer (6 mins); Beaulieu-sur-Mer (10 mins); Monaco (25 mins); Roquebrune (30 mins); Menton (37 mins) and Ventimiglia (52 mins).

Heading west: Cagnes-sur-Mer (17 mins); Antibes (29 mins); Juan-les-Pins (32 mins); Cannes (40 mins) and Grasse (1 hr 9 mins).

Chemins de fer de Provence The trains of this private rail company depart from their own station, a couple of blocks north of Nice-Ville. Their historic Train des Pignes, the 'Pine-Cone Line' (no one knows for

sure where the name comes from) follows the route of the river Var up into the mountains and then swings west to Digne-les-Bains, with plenty of stops in between for those who want to see a mountain village or two and do some walking. The full scenic route takes just over three hours, with four daily trains in each direction. Digne-les-Bains is a quaint, medieval spa town; it's still possible to take the naturally hot waters, which are said to be good for rheumatism. On some weekends from May to October, you can take a special trip along a section of the line on an old steam train; check the timetable on the website under Nice > Digne-les-Bains, then 'Train Vapeur'.
4 bis rue Alfred Binet 04 97 03 80 80 www.trainprovence.com
Tram: Libération

TRIPS BY BUS

Buses depart from Nice's *gare routière* (the central bus station on boulevard Jean Jaurès). Services are run by Ligne d'Azur (see page 58), the bus corporation for the Nice metropolitan area, and the regional TAM (Transport Alpes-Maritimes). Timetables for individual routes are easily found on the Ligne d'Azur website, including the routes covered by TAM. The central bus station is divided into *quais* (platforms, or bays), at which the service numbers and timetables are posted.

Buses will take you to all the places served by the trains, and some that the train doesn't reach. As part of a plan to encourage more people to take the bus, all trips anywhere along the Côte d'Azur are now €1. Bear in mind that buses tend to be much slower than trains, but the ride is generally more scenic and the vehicles are air-conditioned and comfortable.

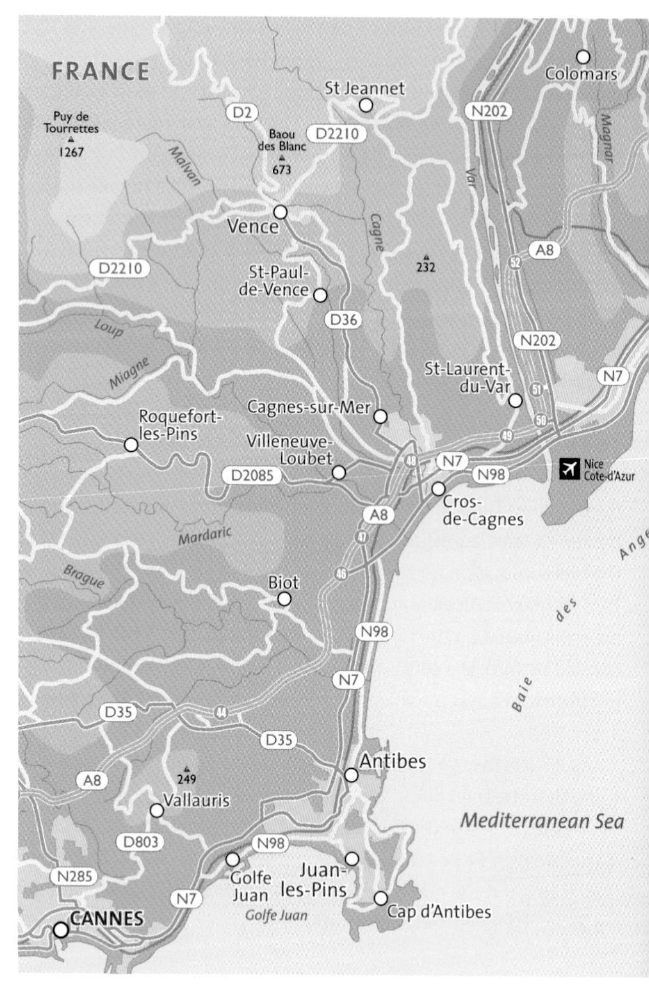
FRANCE
Puy de Tourrettes
1267
Malvan
D2
St Jeannet
Baou des Blanc
673
D2210
N202
Colomars
Magnan
Var
Vence
Cagne
D2210
A8
232
St-Paul-de-Vence
D36
Loup
N202
Miagne
St-Laurent-du-Var
N7
Cagnes-sur-Mer
Roquefort-les-Pins
Villeneuve-Loubet
N7
N98
D2085
Nice Cote-d'Azur
Cros-de-Cagnes
A8
Mardaric
Brague
Biot
Baie des Anges
N98
N7
D35
D35
Antibes
A8
249
Vallauris
Mediterranean Sea
D803
N98
N285
Golfe Juan
Juan-les-Pins
N7
Cap d'Antibes
CANNES
Golfe Juan

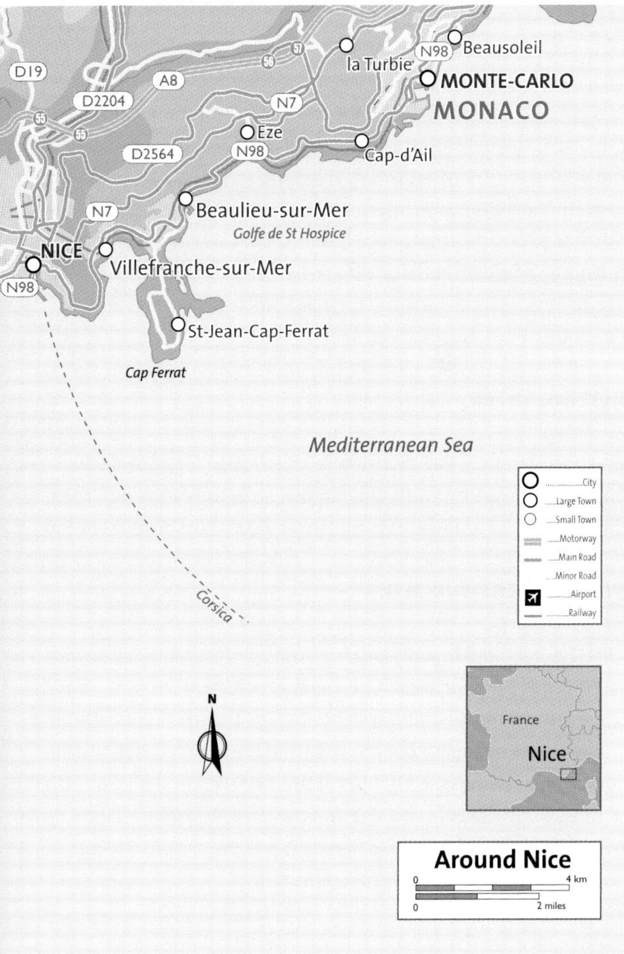
D19
A8
D2204
N7
D2564
N98
Eze
la Turbie
N98
Beausoleil
MONTE-CARLO
MONACO
Cap-d'Ail
Beaulieu-sur-Mer
Golfe de St Hospice
NICE
Villefranche-sur-Mer
N98
St-Jean-Cap-Ferrat
Cap Ferrat
Mediterranean Sea
Corsica
City
Large Town
Small Town
Motorway
Main Road
Minor Road
Airport
Railway
N
France
Nice
Around Nice
0
4 km
0
2 miles

Villefranche, Cap-Ferrat & Beaulieu

Villefranche-sur-Mer (known simply as Villefranche), Beaulieu-sur-Mer (known as Beaulieu) and the town of St-Jean-Cap-Ferrat on the Cap-Ferrat peninsula all lie very close to the city, just east of the promontory of Mont Boron. Villefranche is pretty and historic; St-Jean-Cap-Ferrat is exclusive and upmarket, but the peninsula also has a zoo and good public beaches; Beaulieu is quieter, catering mainly to an older class of visitor. In the area are two other great attractions, Villas Kérylos and Ephrussi. The beaches here tend to be sandier than those in Nice itself.

GETTING THERE

Up to 20 trains per day depart Nice-Ville station for Villefranche and Beaulieu, taking six or ten minutes respectively to reach their destination. For a slower trip but better views, take buses 81 or 100.

VILLEFRANCHE-SUR-MER

This laid-back and friendly small resort is perfect for families, with a picturesque harbour and a safe, sandy beach. Apart from the beach, there are one or two cultural sights, but it's the small town clinging to the slopes by the harbour that is itself the main attraction. The colourful, pastel-washed houses of this fishing port define a warren of narrow, hilly streets and alleyways, with plenty of cafés and restaurants. One street, the covered alley known as rue Obscure, has been dated back to the 13th century.

Tourist office ⓐ Jardin François Binon ⓣ 04 93 01 73 68 ⓦ www.villefranche-sur-mer.fr ⓛ 09.00–19.00 July & Aug;

09.00–12.00, 14.00–18.30 Mon–Sat, June & Sept; 09.00–12.00, 14.00–18.00 Mon–Sat, Jan–May & Oct–mid-Nov; 09.00–12.00, 13.00–17.00 Mon–Sat, mid-Nov–Dec

No shortage of dive boats at Villefranche

SIGHTS & ATTRACTIONS

Chapelle de St-Pierre (St Peter's Chapel)

The quayside possesses a star attraction in this 14th-century fishermen's chapel. The interior was decorated in 1957 by Jean Cocteau with frescoes depicting the life and works of St Peter. ⓐ quai Admiral Courbet ◷ 10.00–12.00, 15.00–19.00 Tues–Sun, June–Sept; 10.00–12.00, 15.00–17.00 Oct–May. Admission charge

La Citadelle & Les Musées de la Citadelle (Citadel & Citadel Museums)

The enormous Citadel was built by the Duke of Savoy in 1554 to defend the Port. Villefranche's deep-water outer harbour or *rade* has been strategically important for centuries; the Duke's galleys were stationed here and their commandant resided in the Palais de Marine on quai Ponchardier. Villefranche remained an important naval base for the French and latterly the US Sixth Fleet until the 1960s, and used to be a rather raunchier place than it is now. Today the Citadel houses several historical and art museums, an open-air theatre and the town hall. There is an entertaining changing of the guard ceremony on the Citadel drawbridge every evening at 19.00 in July and August, at which two Savoyard pikemen in 16th-century uniform are relieved by the French army's Chasseurs Alpins, symbolising the dual military heritage of the fort. ⓣ 04 93 76 33 27 ◷ 10.00–12.00, 14.00–17.00 Wed–Mon, Oct–May; 09.00–12.00, 15.00–18.00 Wed–Mon, June & Sept; 10.00–12.00, 15.00–19.00 Wed–Mon, July & Aug ⓘ closed Nov & Sun mornings

ACTIVITIES

Affrètement Maritime Villefranchois This company runs boat trips of one to two hours around Cap-Ferrat and as far as Monaco and Menton and back (without stopping); it also offers a four-hour

'Mediterranean photo safari' to see dolphins and rorqual and cachalot whales. ⓐ Quayside near pl. Wilson ⓣ 04 93 76 65 65 ⓦ www.amv-sirenes.com ⓛ 4-hour safari 09.30 Wed & Sat, June–Sept; 09.30 Thur, July & Aug; 2-hour Monaco trip 15.00 Wed & Sat, June–Sept; 1-hour Cap-Ferrat trip 17.00 Wed, July & Aug. Booking essential

Aqua Pro Dive International (Centre de Plongée) Exploration diving, photo diving for children, equipment rental and introductions for beginners. ⓐ 16 rue du Poilu ⓣ 04 93 01 71 04 ⓛ Hours & schedules vary; call for times & bookings

Beaches The excellent beach at Villefranche is long and safe for family swimming and provides all the activity many visitors need, but if you prefer to get closer to the Med there are plenty of opportunities at Villefranche for boat trips, whale-watching and diving.

Dark Pelican Hires out a range of motor boats by the afternoon or day. You'll need your passport as proof of identity and will have to leave a hefty deposit in cash or by cheque (not credit card), however. ⓐ Port de la Santé, 1 quai Courbet ⓣ 04 93 01 76 54 ⓦ http://darkpelican.com

RETAIL THERAPY

Brocante & antiques market A weekly market devoted to second-hand items of all kinds and qualities. ⓐ pl. Amélie Pollonais & Jardin Binon ⓛ Sun

Provençal market The colourful weekly produce and craft market is a good place to buy Provençal fabrics, local olives and olive oil, clothes and flowers. ⓐ Jardin Binon ⓛ 08.00–13.00 Sat

TAKING A BREAK

Cafés and ice cream parlours can be found in nearly every street of the Old Town of Villefranche. The comfortable terrace of Beluga in Villefranche (see below) is a particularly good place to sit over a cool drink watching the yachts in the harbour, and if you're serious about boats they keep a rack full of magazines on the subject.

Chez Hiên **£** A wide selection of exotic dishes – Indian and Oriental, Greek and Creole – is served up at this restaurant in the Old Town, just one block behind the waterfront. ⓐ 4 rue du Poilu ⓣ 04 93 01 11 32 ⓦ www.chezhien.com ⓛ 08.00–02.00

Le Cosmo **£–££** Across from the Chapelle St-Pierre, this bar and brasserie is equally convenient for lunch after the Saturday market or a late supper or drink. Salads and seafood are excellent, as is their version of anchoïde, an anchovy and tuna dip, served with an enormous basket of raw vegetables. Note that a more limited menu is available between mealtimes ⓐ 11 pl. Amélie Pollonais ⓣ 04 93 01 84 05 ⓛ 07.00–01.00

Beluga **££** Delicious tapas and a good range of other dishes are the order of the day at this cool restaurant and lounge bar overlooking the seafront. ⓐ 3 quai Ponchardier ⓣ 04 93 80 28 34 ⓛ 12.00–23.00

La Mère Germaine **££** 'Mom' Germaine, 'adopted' by the American Navy officers based in Villefranche, served up traditional French cuisine from 1938 and through much of the 20th century. Today the fantastic restaurant is still family-run. Don't miss the killer wine cellar. ⓐ 9 quai Admiral Courbet ⓣ 04 93 01 71 39 ⓦ www.meregermaine.com ⓛ 12.00–14.30, 19.00–21.30 (until 22.00, July & Aug)

Take in the buzz of the quayside at Villefranche

ACCOMMODATION

Given the short journey time and frequency of the trains, staying in Villefranche and visiting Nice by day is a viable option, especially if you're travelling as a family and want to spend plenty of time on the town's sandy beach. Most options are on or near the main highway, the Moyenne Corniche, about 10–15 minutes' walk from the town centre.

Fiancée du Pirate £–££ This splendidly named representative of the reliable Logis de France association has good-value rooms for families of four. It's quite a way from the town centre, but a good option if you have your own wheels. ⓐ 8 blvd de la Corne d'Or ⓣ 04 93 76 67 40 ⓦ www.fianceedupirate.com

La Flore £–££ Another Logis member, in a renovated 19th-century building, with excellent views onto the harbour of Villefranche.

Cap-Ferrat has some of the best beaches on the Riviera

Good restaurant, too. ⓐ 5 blvd Princesse Grace de Monaco ⓣ 04 93 76 30 30 ⓦ www.hotel-la-flore.fr

ST-JEAN-CAP-FERRAT

Cap-Ferrat's green peninsula has been famous for its millionaires' villas since European society started to buy up the real estate in the 19th century, but you won't see much of them beyond their high security gates. If you arrive by bus 81 from Nice you can enjoy a panoramic circuit of the cape, but the more active will find that the 14 km (9 mile) coastal path is a walker's paradise. The Port of St-Jean, once a fishing village and now a harbour full of upmarket yachts, is a pleasant place for a drink or lunch. There are plenty of minor delights for walkers to discover, including the Chapelle St-Hospice and the lighthouse at the southern tip of the cape.

The **tourist information office** has its own bus stop and is a good starting point, midway between St-Jean and the Zoo. ⓐ 59 av. Denis

Séméria ⓣ 04 93 76 51 00 ⓦ www.ville-saint-jean-cap-ferrat.fr
Bus: 81 (which stops at all the sights on the Cap)

SIGHTS & ATTRACTIONS

Villa Ephrussi de Rothschild

More correctly called the Villa Ile de France, this beautiful pink and white confection off the Basse Corniche was built at the beginning of the 20th century. Béatrice Ephrussi de Rothschild was born into a wealthy banking family and spent much of her fortune collecting works of art and antiques to fill the villa she had built. On her death in 1934 the villa was bequeathed to the Institut de France, who now own it. Her real enthusiasm was for the 18th century, which is reflected especially in the priceless porcelain collection. For once, the cliché 'treasure trove' is fully justified; you don't have to be an antiques or art enthusiast to be overwhelmed. The gardens are immaculate, too.

The gardens of Villa Ephrussi are an attraction in their own right

The **Les Azuriales opera festival** (www.azuriales-opera.com), held at the Villa Ephrussi de Rothschild for two weeks during August, has been a major event since 1997. Off av. Denis Semeria at entrance to St-Jean-Cap-Ferrat 04 93 01 33 09 www.villa-ephrussi.com 10.00–18.00 1st wk Jan & mid-Feb–early Nov; 14.00–18.00 Mon–Fri, 10.00–18.00 Sat & Sun, mid-Jan–mid-Feb & early Nov–Dec. Admission charge

Zoo-Parc Cap-Ferrat

This zoo is home to 300 animals and birds, including bears, tigers, monkeys and zebras, and will please younger holidaymakers. 117 blvd du Général de Gaulle 04 93 76 07 60 www.zoocapferrat.com. Admission charge

ACTIVITIES

Aside from walking and enjoying the lush scenery, Cap-Ferrat also offers some very nice public beaches. Passable Plage is a short walk from the tourist office along the chemin de Passable; Paloma Plage is about 1 km (⅔ mile) south from the port of St-Jean, heading towards the Pointe St-Hospice, and there's another beach just north of the Port. Cafés and ice cream parlours can be found near the marina.

BEAULIEU-SUR-MER

The name means 'beautiful place' (according to legend, it was coined by Napoleon when he first laid eyes on it) and the attractions of the site were apparent to the ancient Greek mariners who founded the town. At the end of the 19th century American millionaire and newspaper proprietor Gordon Bennett discovered this tiny fishing village and developed it into a resort for wealthy belle époque visitors, including Edward, Prince of Wales and Gustave Eiffel. Much of the elegant architecture dates from this time, and the town still retains a genteel air. It's the ambience rather than individual sights that attracts visitors, but there are plenty of photogenic buildings, including the Casino and the Chapelle Sancta Maria de Olivo. **Tourist office** ⓐ pl. Clémenceau ⓣ 04 93 01 02 21 ⓦ www.ot-beaulieu-sur-mer.fr ⓛ 09.00–12.30, 14.00–19.00 Mon-Sat, 09.00–12.30 Sun, summer; 09.00–12.15, 14.00–18.00 Mon–Fri, 09.00–12.15, 1400–17.00 Sat, winter

SIGHTS & ATTRACTIONS

Villa Kérylos

Just outside Beaulieu stands the 'sister' of the Villa Ephrussi, the Villa Kérylos, also owned by the Institut de France and also the life's work of one obsessive individual. The archaeologist Théodore Reinach was the scion of another wealthy banking family prominent in late 19th-century France. He was inspired to re-create his vision of a patrician Greek palace that stood on the island of Delos in the second century BC, and entrusted the building of his dream villa to an architect who shared his love of archaeology, Emmanuel Pontremoli.

The Villa took six years to construct, following as closely as possible the layout of the remains uncovered on Delos. It was always intended as a house to live in, and the interior, although faithful to the appearance of a classical Greek villa, incorporated all the modern conveniences of the time, cleverly disguised. Today it is a tour de force that delights thousands of visitors. Be sure to pick up a free audio guide to get the most out of your visit. ⓐ Impasse Gustave Eiffel ⓣ 04 93 01 01 44 ⓦ www.villa-kerylos.com ⓛ 10.00–18.00 1st wk Jan & mid-Feb–early Nov; 14.00–18.00 Mon–Fri, 10.00–18.00 Sat & Sun, mid-Jan–mid-Feb & early Nov–Dec

CULTURE & ENTERTAINMENT

Beaulieu hosts a very full programme of concerts and other performances during the summer months – you can get up-to-date details from the tourist office and its website. A regular favourite are the Nuits Guitares in the Jardin de l'Olivaie. If you've caught the roulette bug in Nice, Beaulieu has its own historic and upmarket casino – check Ⓦ www.casinobeaulieu.com for further information.

ACTIVITIES

Beaulieu has two very pleasant beaches, the Baie des Fourmis (*fourmis* means 'ants', but don't worry, it refers to the little black rocks that dot the area) and the Petite Afrique. Cafés and ice cream parlours can be found near the marina.

RETAIL THERAPY

Beaulieu avoids designer labels and prefers individual small boutiques. As a result, it's well worth looking out for classic rather than youth-oriented fashions.

TAKING A BREAK

African Queen ££ Solid brasserie and pizzeria fare, but a cut above the average in terms of quality. A favourite spot with celebrities – the chance of stargazing alone is well worth the visit. Ⓐ Port de Plaisance Ⓣ 04 93 01 10 85 Ⓦ http://africanqueen.fr Ⓛ 12.00–00.00

Les Agaves ££–£££ High-end French cuisine, served up in a formal atmosphere in Beaulieu's Palais des Anglais. Try the roasted duck, or their speciality, homemade country pâté. Reservations essential. Ⓐ 4 av. Maréchal Foch Ⓣ 04 93 01 13 12 Ⓦ www.lesagaves.com Ⓛ 19.00–22.00; closed 1st 2 wks of Dec

Eze

Eze is well worth a half-day trip from Nice; it is the archetypal *village perché*, an ancient and pretty township sitting 429 m (1407 ft) above sea level, with stunning views out to the Mediterranean. More than half a day would be spreading its charms too thinly, unless you plan to use the remainder of your time soaking up the sun in Eze-sur-Mer, the neighbouring seaside village at the foot of the precipice. However, to get from one to the other involves waiting for a bus or a long walk down (only fitness fanatics would do the two places in reverse order). The footpath is clearly signposted and is named after Nietzsche, the German philosopher who used to climb it in the 1880s. It is steep in parts and the steps, where there are any, are quite deep. The advertised time for the descent is 45 minutes, but allow an hour on a hot summer's day.

As at many Mediterranean coastal sites, the population of Eze has moved periodically from coast to hill and back again according to the safety of the times. The Celts inhabited the hilltop village 2,000 years ago. The Romans, living in a more secure age, founded the port of Avisio on the coast; then the Dark Ages brought raids from Moorish pirates, driving the inhabitants to re-fortify the hill – the walls and gates of Eze date from the 14th century. In the 1880s Eze was 'discovered' by Friedrich Nietzsche and from the 1920s to the 1950s was the home of Prince William of Sweden, whose villa is now a luxury hotel. In more recent times Eze has seen an influx of celebrity visitors, ranging from President Clinton and Walt Disney (a frequent guest of the Hôtel Chèvre d'Or) to Tina Turner and Naomi Campbell.

GETTING THERE

The best way to see the two sides of Eze in one day is by bus to Eze Village, then by bus (or on foot down the path) to Eze-sur-Mer, with a final short ride by train from Eze-sur-Mer back to Nice. From the *gare routière* in Nice (see page 51), take either bus 83 or 112. There is a bus approximately every 90 minutes on most days, starting around 07.20; the journey to Eze Village takes about 20 minutes, depending on traffic. The route takes the Moyenne Corniche – be sure to sit on the right-hand side of the bus for the best views on the outward journey. The final approach to the village is over an impressive early 20th-century viaduct, known locally as the Pont du Diable ('Devil's Bridge'; according to legend, the bridge-builder narrowly avoided selling his soul to the Devil).

To get from Eze Village to Eze-sur-Mer, take bus 83; buses should run every 20 minutes and take around 25 minutes to reach their destination, but it's best to check timetables in advance. The 15-minute return journey by train from Eze-sur-Mer back to Nice goes along the coast, but there are no great views.

Tourist office ⓐ pl. du Général de Gaulle, near the bus stop ⓣ 04 93 41 26 00 ⓦ www.eze-riviera.com ⓛ 09.00–19.00 Apr–Oct; 09.00–18.30 Mon–Sat, Nov–Mar

SIGHTS & ATTRACTIONS

It's a short walk up into the Old Town, the original fortified village once topped by a castle that was destroyed in Louis XIV's time, through the medieval Postern Gate. The unforced charm of the narrow pedestrian-only streets, and the views out to sea and across to the Alpes-Maritimes, are hard to beat. As has often been remarked,

PULLING POWER

Until it became fashionable after World War II Eze was still an agricultural commune and the only feasible means of transport along its steep narrow lanes was the donkey. Two of the Provençal breed of donkeys, Nani and Nina, until recently took luggage up to the Hôtel Château Eza; they can now be admired in their retirement stable outside the walls.

it would be difficult to take a bad photograph in Eze, unless it was spoilt by other tourists getting in the picture. You have to accept that many other people have been attracted by the same sights as you, and the alleys can get a little crowded (so plan to arrive as early as the buses will let you). Unfortunately for today's tourists, the 14th-century builders of the stronghold planned the narrow streets deliberately to slow down the advance of invaders.

The oldest building in Eze is the Chapelle de Saint-Croix (also known as the Chapelle des Pénitents Blancs, or Chapel of the White Penitents) of 1306. The medieval mansions of Eze's wealthier residents have now become luxury hotels, including the Chèvre d'Or and the Château Eza (see page 131). The church of Notre Dame de l'Assomption was designed by the Italian architect Antonio Spinelli between 1764 and 1778 to replace an old ruined one. The exterior is relatively plain, but inside Spinelli let loose with a riot of *trompe-l'œil*, real windows on one side being matched by fake ones on the other, a false pulpit paired with a real one, and so on; this is baroque at its most theatrical.

At the very summit of Eze is the **Jardin Exotique** (ⓐ rue du Château ⓣ 04 93 41 10 30 ⓛ 09.00–20.00 July & Aug; 09.00–19.00 June & Sept; 09.00–18.30 May & Oct; 09.00–18.00 Apr; 09.30–17.30 Mar; 09.30–17.00

Nov–Feb. Admission charge), begun in 1949 by the then-mayor on the site of the old castle. Its collection of cacti and other dry-climate plants is complemented by female statuary by Jean-Philippe Richard, placed in strategic locations to enhance (or detract from, depending on your taste) the stunning views over Cap-Ferrat and the Italian coast. An orientation table lets you work out whether it is really possible to see Corsica, as is claimed. Whether or not you like succulents or statues, the panoramas are worth the entry fee.

The seaside part of the town, Eze-sur-Mer (also known as Eze Bord-de-Mer), has some good beaches, mostly supervised by lifeguards, and a few cafés and restaurants, as well as the railway station on the main Nice–Ventimiglia line.

RETAIL THERAPY

The old citadel streets are filled with shops selling antiques, craft items and art (both originals and prints). Prices are as you would expect in a place visited by so many tourists, but much of the merchandise is of a better quality than the average tourist trap. In the more modern part of the village are two very popular outlets:

La Cristallerie d'Eze This shop (a branch of a company based in the northern French crystal centre of Baccarat) does a nice line in crystalware gifts, ranging from wine glasses to chess sets to jewellery and objets d'art. ⓐ pl. Général de Gaulle ⓣ 04 93 41 20 34 ⓑ 10.30–19.00 Mon–Sat

Fragonard The famous fragrance company has a large factory-laboratory just off the main road, at which you can take a multilingual guided tour of the science and craft of perfume-making before

visiting the boutique, which stocks a wide range of antique jewellery, embroidered household linen, traditional quilted Provençal *boutis*, glassware and wickerwork, preserves, perfumes, natural aromatic oils and other products. ⓐ Moyenne Corniche ⓣ 04 93 41 05 05 ⓦ www.fragonard.com ⓛ Factory: 08.30–18.30; boutique: 10.00–19.00 ⓘ closes for 2 hrs over lunch in winter

TAKING A BREAK

Most cafés and lunch stops congregate in place de la Collette, at the foot of the Old Town, near the bus stop. All of them are perfect for a drink or simple meal while you're waiting for your bus to Eze-sur-Mer or back to Nice.

RESTAURANTS

The best restaurants in Eze are those attached to the luxury hotels that cling to the hillside – see under Accommodation. Lunch at one of these need not break the bank, if you're happy to choose from one of the set menus; dinner is always a leisurely gourmet affair and priced accordingly. For the more modest end of the scale, head for place de la Collette at the base of the citadel.

Le Cactus £ An excellent little restaurant, serving crêpes, sandwiches and salads at a fraction of the cost compared with nearby swish locales. Dine on the terrace to enjoy the amazing views. ⓐ La Placette ⓣ 04 93 41 19 02 ⓛ 11.00–22.00 summer; 11.00–22.00 Sat & Sun, winter ⓘ closed Jan

Cheval Blanc £ Slightly better value than some of its companions. The menu is mainly pizza, standard Italian dishes and salads.

ⓐ pl. de la Collette ⓣ 04 93 41 03 17 ⓒ 12.00–15.00, 19.00–22.30 Thur–Tues, Jan–Nov

Sample savoury cuisine in Eze's Michelin-starred restaurants

Restaurant le Troubadour ££ In contrast to the haute cuisine of the château hotels and the mass-market offerings of the budget restaurants, this rustic establishment serves authentic and traditional Provençal fare. ⓐ 4 rue du Brec ⓣ 04 93 41 19 03 ◔ 12.00–14.30, 19.00–22.30

Château Eza ££–£££ Michelin-starred cuisine from chef Axel Wagner includes two lunchtime '*Menus saveur*' that are reasonably priced considering their outstanding quality, and a choice of light meals in the afternoon. ⓐ rue de la Pise ⓣ 04 93 41 12 24 ⓦ www.chateaueza.com ◔ 12.00–14.30, 19.00–22.00

Château de la Chèvre d'Or £££ Opinions vary on whether this or the Château Eza is Eze's leader in the restaurant stakes, but Philippe Labbé's handling of Mediterranean cuisine has many fans. ⓐ Moyenne Corniche, rue du Barri ⓣ 04 92 10 66 66 ⓦ www.chevredor.com ◔ 12.30–14.30, 19.00–22.00 mid-Mar–Oct

ACCOMMODATION

Eze's popularity with the rich and famous has resulted in some of the most luxurious hotels on the Côte d'Azur. However, cheaper accommodation can be found in the area, including B&Bs and *gîtes*, if you don't mind staying a little way from the Old Town. The tourist office can provide a comprehensive list of all the options. A car is essential if you want to use Eze as a base for extensive sightseeing on the Riviera, though.

Auberge le Soleil £ This villa-style accommodation on the Basse Corniche in Eze-sur-Mer is very close to the sea and has eight comfortable en-suite guest rooms. The good on-site restaurant makes half-board a reasonable option. ⓐ 44 av. Liberté ⓣ 04 93 01 51 46 ⓦ www.auberge-lesoleil.com

La Bastide aux Camélias ££ A charming B&B just outside Eze village, with four rooms, a swimming pool, sauna and gardens. All rooms now include free breakfast and use of the hammam and Jacuzzi. ⓐ 23C route de l'Adret ⓣ 04 93 41 13 68 ⓦ www.bastideauxcamelias.com ⓒ Jan–Nov

Cap Estel £££ For utter extravagance (if you haven't had enough already) and total exclusivity, book a room or suite at Cap Estel, on the shores of Eze-sur-Mer. Former home of a Russian prince, the five-acre estate on a private peninsula has undergone a huge restoration and is now a luxury villa with stunning rooms. ⓐ 1312 av. Raymond Poincaré ⓣ 04 93 76 29 29 ⓦ www.capestel.com ⓒ Mar–Dec

Château de la Chèvre d'Or £££ The 24-room Relais & Châteaux hotel, a conversion of several medieval houses in the Old Town, has hosted many celebrity visitors, including Walt Disney, who used to be a frequent guest here. In addition to two swimming pools, stunning views and all the usual top-flight facilities, it boasts three restaurants. ⓐ Moyenne Corniche, rue du Barri ⓣ 04 92 10 66 66 ⓦ www.chevredor.com ⓒ Mid-Mar–Oct

Château Eza £££ The former home of Prince William of Sweden, this fashionable clifftop hotel has just ten rooms. It perfectly combines an authentic medieval setting with modern facilities and unmatchable views over the sea. ⓐ rue de la Pise ⓣ 04 93 41 12 24 ⓦ www.chateaueza.com ⓒ Mid-Dec–Oct

St-Paul-de-Vence

St-Paul is another fortified hilltop village beloved of artists, tourists and celebrities. Lying to the west of Nice and some way inland, it doesn't have the sea views of Eze, but the old village inside the medieval walls is larger and the streets a little wider, so even when it gets busy in summer it feels a little less crowded. It also possesses an extra major attraction in the shape of the Fondation Maeght, one of the world's most important collections of modern art, contained in a purpose-built gallery set in an attractive hillside garden.

In the Middle Ages, St-Paul-de-Vence was important enough to be fortified by the kings of France, but by the beginning of the 20th century had become a rural backwater. After World War I it attracted the attention of some of the most illustrious artists of the time, including Picasso, Modigliani, Matisse, Braque and Dufy, all of whom paid for lodging at the (then) humble inn of the Colombe d'Or with their paintings, many of which still hang there. From these beginnings it became a centre of modern art and art dealers and latterly a major tourist destination.

GETTING THERE

Bus 400 departs from quai 5 in Nice's central bus station approximately hourly every day, including public holidays. The journey to St-Paul-de-Vence takes about 45 mins, passing through Cagnes-sur-Mer (about 20 mins from Nice) and continuing on to the town of Vence (about 1 hour from Nice). Bus 94 will take you to Vence and Cagnes-sur-Mer, but it bypasses St-Paul.

Away from the main shopping streets you can have St-Paul to yourself

DAY TRIPPING
Cagnes-sur-Mer, Haute Cagnes (the old medieval town) and Vence are all worthy destinations in their own right; it is possible to combine a half-day in St-Paul with a visit to one of these (to attempt more than two in a day would be stretching it). You can also catch a train from Nice-Ville station to Cagnes-sur-Mer but not the other destinations.

SIGHTS & ATTRACTIONS

The bus stops outside the tiny medieval Chapelle de Ste-Claire on the main road. From there it is a short walk past the Colombe d'Or, now a luxury hotel rather than the humble inn of yesteryear, into place de Gaulle. On your right is the large *boules* pitch, which hosts regional tournaments and celebrity matches from time to time. At the far end of place de Gaulle you come to the main gate of the fortified town, from which leads the principal street, rue Grande. The tourist office is located on your immediate right. If the street is already a little crowded, it's better to carry on past the main gate and make a complete circuit of the ramparts, which hold great views over the countryside in all directions. At various intervals you can dive into the town through the narrow connecting streets.

Despite the numbers of visitors, and the obvious commercialisation, which has turned almost every ancient house into an art gallery or purveyor of designer chocolates and olive oils, the maze of flower-bedecked streets retains an irresistible charm. Halfway along, rue Grande opens out to accommodate the Grande Fontaine of 1850, for a long time the town's main water supply (always a problem in the mountains); the water is not drinkable now. The Eglise Collégiale, the church at the top of the Old Town, dates from the 13th century and has an atmospheric interior combining medieval and baroque elements. Facing it across the square is the *Mairie* or town hall, occupying the 12th-century keep of the original castle; next door is the town's museum, the **Musée d'Histoire Locale** (10.00–18.00 Mon–Fri, 15.00–18.00 Sat & Sun, Dec–Oct). At the far end of rue Grande and through the porte de Nice, which cuts through the ramparts, lies the town cemetery, which contains the grave of Marc Chagall (see page 100), who died here in 1985.

The small but very helpful **tourist office** (2 rue Grande 04 93 32 86 95 www.saint-pauldevence.com 10.00–19.00 June–Sept; 10.00–18.00 Oct–May) just inside the main gate of the town has good maps and brochures on accommodation and shopping, and offers guided tours; they also rent out sets of *boules* for a game on St-Paul's famous pitch (see left).

At the Fondation Maeght the garden is an art gallery, too

CULTURE

Fondation Maeght

This world-class art gallery is a stiff 20-minute uphill walk from near the bus stop at Chapelle Ste-Claire. If you have your own car it's not a problem to drive up and use the car park at the gallery; otherwise, older and less agile visitors might find the trek difficult and would be well advised to take a taxi from the stand near the Colombe d'Or.

Aimé Maeght came to the south of France as a Belgian war orphan in 1914 and later opened an art gallery in Cannes. He and his wife Marguerite became friends of most of the leading exponents of art in the inter-war years in France, including Bonnard, Matisse, Braque, Mirò, Calder and Giacometti, and through their other gallery in Paris helped to promote their work. In 1964 they set up a private foundation to which they donated their own extensive collection, and the Fondation now owns more than 9,000 works by world-famous modern artists (although they're never all on display at the same time). The striking modern gallery was designed by Catalan architect Josep Luis Sert, and the surrounding garden is decorated with typically quirky figures by Mirò and Giacometti. There is no set route through the gallery and no particular plan of arrangement of the ever-changing exhibits, all of which makes the experience one of personal discovery rather than art education. ⓐ Montée des Trious, St-Paul-de-Vence ⓣ 04 93 32 81 63 ⓦ www.maeght.com ◔ 10.00–19.00 July–Sept; 10.00–18.00 Oct–June. Admission charge

RETAIL THERAPY

If you're seriously contemplating acquiring an original work of art, then you could spend a day in the commercial galleries of St-Paul. Try **Galerie**

du Vieux St-Paul (ⓐ 16 rue Grande) for a good mix of established and lesser-known artists. The town's shops are also strong on furniture, ceramics and other objects of interior design, while other boutiques specialise in figurines, traditional garments and other gifts with a Provençal air. The accent is mostly on authentic, quality goods at a commensurate price, rather than cheap souvenirs, so bring your credit card! The tourist office issues a comprehensive catalogue of local shops to help you find what you're looking for. In addition, there is a small Provençal produce market near the *boules* arena at the entrance to the town on Tuesdays and Thursdays, and on Saturday mornings the same spot overflows with both produce and flowers.

There's plenty to tempt the shopper in St-Paul-de-Vence

TAKING A BREAK

Fine food at fine prices is not hard to come by in the restaurants of the luxury hotels in and around St-Paul. Luckily, there's also no shortage of simpler establishments good for a morning coffee, cooling drink or simple lunch.

Dolce Italia £ If you've made the climb up the steps to the church you're probably ready for one of the true Italian cappuccinos or ice creams that this café specialises in. ⓐ 13 pl. de l'Eglise ⓣ 04 93 24 09 95 ⓛ 11.00–19.00

Malabar £ Calling itself a 'gourmet snack bar', this café on the ramparts serves good-value sandwiches, *pissaladière* and other snacks, and lunches, all to take away or eat on the spot. Everything served is homemade. ⓐ 7 Rempart Ouest ⓣ 04 93 32 60 14 ⓛ 12.00–15.30 Thur–Tues

Le Tilleul £–££ This busy terrace restaurant is just inside the walls to the left of the town gate. The food is unsophisticated but tasty and service is efficient. In summer it attracts wandering entertainers – children will love it. ⓐ pl. du Tilleul ⓣ 04 93 32 80 36 ⓦ www.letilleul-saintpaul.com ⓛ 10.00–22.00

Le Saint Paul £££ Mediterranean food doesn't come any better than the Michelin-starred cuisine on the flowery terrace of this Relais & Château hotel. ⓐ 80 rue Grande ⓣ 04 93 32 62 25 ⓦ www.lesaintpaul.com ⓛ 12.30–13.45, 19.30–21.45, Apr–Oct; 12.30–13.45, 19.30–21.45 Fri–Tues, Feb–Mar & Nov–Dec ⓘ closed Jan–early Feb

EVENTS

The local tourist authority works hard to make sure its visitors don't become bored, with a full programme of events ranging from summer concerts to the folk festival Fête Patronale de Ste-Claire – three days of traditional costumes, dancing and processions at the beginning of August. This is followed closely by four days of *pétanque* competitions that attract devotees from as far afield as Japan. Autumn sees a heritage weekend in September and the annual festival of the local wine harvest in October. The tourist office issues good seasonal lists of all the organised activities in St-Paul.

ACTIVITIES

St-Paul is a good centre for walking in the surrounding hills, with marked trails leading from near the Chapelle Ste-Claire on the main road. If you've never played *pétanque*, you can learn from a local on the town's famous arena with one of the instruction packages from the tourist office (see page 135).

ACCOMMODATION

St-Paul has plenty of luxury accommodation to suit its celebrity visitors. More cost-wise travellers will find lodgings further out of town, but even if you're not travelling by car it won't matter too much, as most are close to the main bus route.

Hostellerie les Remparts £–££ One of the few hotels right in the middle of the Old Town, this traditional stone-built house, with nine

guest rooms and a good regional restaurant, offers a warm welcome. ⓐ 72 rue Grande ⓣ 04 93 32 09 88 ⓦ www.hostellerielesremparts.com

Hôtel le Hameau **££** Within walking distance of the town and the Fondation Maeght, this charming hotel had Chagall as a guest many years ago. It has 17 comfortable rooms and a large swimming pool – and the breakfast marmalade is made with oranges grown on the premises. ⓐ 528 route de la Colle ⓣ 04 93 32 80 24 ⓦ www.le-hameau.com ⓒ closed mid-Nov–mid-Feb

Les Vergers de Saint Paul **££–£££** The 15 rooms and 2 suites here are grouped in a two-storey and a one-storey building around the large central swimming pool. In a secluded location, but less than 1 km (2/3 mile) from the town. ⓐ 940 route de la Colle ⓣ 04 93 32 94 24 ⓦ www.vergersdesaintpaul.com

La Colombe d'Or **£££** What was a simple country inn at the time the artists descended on St-Paul has become a destination hotel and restaurant that is proud of its celebrity guests and the works of art that decorate the place (donated in lieu of payment by the likes of Modigliani and Picasso). The atmosphere is both professional and relaxed – don't expect the service to be stiff or overly pampering. You must be a guest of the hotel or restaurant in order to view their amazing art collection. ⓐ pl. de Gaulle ⓣ 04 93 32 80 02 ⓦ www.la-colombe-dor.com ⓒ closed Nov–beginning of Christmas season

➤ *Gare Nice-Ville is the rail hub of the Riviera*

PRACTICAL
information

Directory

GETTING THERE

By air

Nice-Côte d'Azur airport (see page 50) serves flights from many UK and Irish airlines, including **Aer Lingus** (from Dublin, Cork and London Gatwick ⓣ 08 21 23 02 67 ⓦ www.aerlingus.com), **British Airways** (ⓣ 08 25 82 54 00 ⓦ www.britishairways.com), **British Midland** (ⓣ 01 41 91 87 04 ⓦ www.flybmi.com) and **Bmibaby** (from Birmingham and East Midlands ⓣ 08 90 71 00 81 ⓦ www.bmibaby.com), **easyJet** (from London Gatwick, Luton and Stansted, Bristol, Liverpool, Newcastle and Belfast ⓣ 08 26 10 33 20 ⓦ www.easyjet.com), **Ryanair** (from Dublin ⓣ 08 92 23 23 75 ⓦ www.ryanair.com) and **Globespan** (from Edinburgh ⓣ +44 870 056 6611 ⓦ www.flyglobespan.com). Flight time from London is about two hours.

Airlines operating direct flights from other countries include **Air Transat** (from Montréal, Canada ⓣ 08 25 12 02 48 ⓦ www.airtransat.ca) and **Delta** (from New York, USA ⓣ 08 11 64 00 05 ⓦ www.delta.com).

Many people are aware that air travel emits CO_2, which contributes to climate change. You may be interested in the possibility of lessening the environmental impact of your flight through the charity **Climate Care** (ⓦ www.climatecare.org), which offsets your CO_2 by funding environmental projects around the world.

By rail

The journey from London St Pancras to Paris Gare du Nord on the Eurostar and then by TGV from Paris Gare de Lyon to Nice-Ville averages about nine hours, and return fares can be cheaper than those of many low-cost airlines. If you are Inter-railing or Eurailing, you can reach Nice not only from cities in France but also by direct international trains. The monthly *Thomas Cook European Rail Timetable* has up-to-date schedules for European international and national train services.

Eurostar Ⓣ (UK) 08705 186 186 Ⓦ www.eurostar.com

General rail information Ⓦ www.raileurope.com

Thomas Cook European Rail Timetable Ⓣ (UK) 01733 416477; (USA) 1 800 322 3834 Ⓦ www.thomascookpublishing.com

By road

If you're coming by car from the UK via Calais, it will take you between two and three days to cover the 1,200 km (745 miles) from Calais to Nice.. Head for Marseilles and pick up the A8 *autoroute*, 'La Provençale', to Nice. For the approaches to Nice, see page 54.

ENTRY FORMALITIES

Passports are needed by UK visitors and all others except EU citizens who can produce a national identity card. Visits of up to three months do not require a visa if your nationality is UK, Republic of Ireland, US, Canadian, Australian or New Zealand. Other travellers should consult the French embassy or tourist office in their own country on visa requirements. Ⓦ www.diplomatie.gouv.fr

When going to France, residents of the UK, Ireland and other EU countries may bring personal possessions and goods for personal use, including a reasonable amount of tobacco and alcohol, provided they have been bought in the EU. There are few formalities at the point of entry into France. Residents of non-EU countries, and EU residents arriving from a non-EU country, may bring in up to 400 cigarettes and 50 cigars or 50 g (2 oz) tobacco; 2 litres (3 bottles) of wine and 1 litre (approx. 2 pints) of spirits or liqueurs. The full regulations and definitions of 'reasonable amount' may be checked at Ⓦ www.douane.gouv.fr.

MONEY

The euro (€) is the official currency in France. €1 = 100 cents. It comes in notes of €5, €10, €20, €50, €100, €200 and €500. Coins are in denominations of €1 and €2, and 1, 2, 5, 10, 20 and 50 cents. ATM machines can be found at the airport, railway stations, shopping centres and outside most banks, and they accept most British and international debit and credit cards. They are the quickest and most convenient way to obtain cash, though a charge will be levied. Instructions on use are available in English and other major European languages.

The most widely accepted credit cards are VISA and MasterCard, though other major credit cards such as American Express are also commonly accepted in restaurants and shops. Traveller's cheques have become relatively difficult to cash – seek out a bureau de change, such as the one opposite Galeries Lafayette on avenue Jean Médecin. Foreign money can be cashed at most banks and bureaux de change in Nice, though you may have to produce your passport or other ID.

There is an **American Express** bureau de change (t 04 93 21 59 79 ⌚ 07.00–21.00) at Terminal 1 of Nice Airport. Alternatively, try **Change Mediterranée** in the centre (a 17 av. Jean Médecin t 04 93 87 99 72 ⌚ 08.30–19.00 Mon–Fri, 10.00–17.00 Sat, June–Sept; 08.30–18.00 Mon–Fri, Oct–May).

HEALTH, SAFETY & CRIME

Tap water is safe to drink (if not it is marked *eau non potable*) but the French and most visitors prefer to consume one of the many brands of mineral water.

Medical facilities in France are of an excellent standard, but expensive – ensure you have a European Health Insurance Card

(EHIC) and adequate travel insurance. Most minor ailments can be taken to pharmacies, indicated by a green cross sign – the one in rue Masséna pedestrian zone is open 24 hours. Pharmacies have expert staff who are qualified to offer medical advice and dispense a wide range of medicines. Many drugs, such as aspirin, that are widely available in the UK are obtainable only at pharmacies in France.

Nice is a safe city, by and large. The beach and the streets west and north of the promenade des Anglais are not the best places to be late at night (and budget travellers should never be tempted to sleep overnight on the beach to save on accommodation costs). Otherwise, take normal sensible precautions – avoid deserted

Rue Masséna's pharmacy is always open

streets by night, keep valuables secure from pickpockets and opportunist bag-snatchers by day. Never leave valuables in a car, as theft from (and of) automobiles is one of Nice's main crime issues. You may encounter one of the hustlers who especially frequent the seafront. A common scam is to 'give' you a worthless ring or trinket and then as the conversation drags on ask for payment of 'whatever you think it is worth'. There are also plausible 'distressed tourists' around – some quite elderly – who will spin you a heartbreaking story of being suddenly penniless and not being able even to phone their consulate. In both cases, simply walking away is normally sufficient to deter the scam operators. Public disorder and drunkenness are rare – so rare that people stand and stare at the occasional drunks (who embarrassingly tend to be foreigners in the Old Town).

OPENING HOURS

Shops tend to open 09.00–12.00 and 14.00–19.00 Monday to Saturday, although those in the main pedestrian areas tend to stay open later and don't close for lunch. Banks open 08.30–12.00 and 13.30–17.00 Monday to Friday. Note that some museums are closed on Mondays.

TOILETS

Museums generally have good toilet facilities. The average café and restaurant toilet is clean but small and often unisex; the better the establishment, the better the facilities. If you want to use the facilities in cafés, bars and restaurants, you generally have to buy something first. Public toilets in Nice are the modern, hygienic coin-operated cubicles (which young children shouldn't be allowed to use unaccompanied).

CHILDREN

The only health threat to children on the Riviera is the strength of the sun – ensure that they have adequate protection from it at all times. If you are travelling with babies or young children you can buy nappies, baby food and other supplies in supermarkets and pharmacies. Restaurants are used to children eating with the family, and junior menus and smaller portions are commonly offered. Many attractions and transport providers have reduced rates for children.

There is plenty to keep the kids entertained in Nice and on the Riviera generally. The most obvious attraction is the beach – the sandy beaches of Villefranche and Cap-Ferrat, in particular. In Nice, the carousel in the Jardin Albert 1er facing the seafront will keep kids amused for a while, as will the 'human statue' street entertainers in rue Masséna pedestrian area (though they're perhaps a bit scary for the very young). It's worth visiting the Château, too: there's a playground on top of the hill, and a puppet show on the Château's main esplanade every Sunday afternoon (16.00–17.00). A ride on the Petit Train Touristique (see page 59) is loved by children and parents alike; the Castel des Deux Rois mini-amusement park in eastern Nice, between the Port and Terra Amata (see page 101), also has its own *petit train*, along with mini-golf, a giant chessboard, wooden play huts and more. For animal fun, head to the Zoo-Parc Cap-Ferrat (see page 121). There's also a theme park in the area:

Marineland: Parc de la Mer et de l'Aventure This theme park is just a short train ride away near Antibes. In addition to the Wild West area, an aquasplash and adventure golf, the family can enjoy performing dolphins that can be petted, a pirate ship that lets you get close up to orcas, a scary shark tunnel and a tropical aquarium. ⓐ Off the N7 route national ⓣ 08 92 30 06 06 ⓦ www.marineland.fr ⓒ 10.00–22.30 mid-Feb–Dec ⓡ Train from Nice-Ville to Biot, then five-minute walk

COMMUNICATIONS

Internet

Even some smaller hotels provide an internet connection, but in any case internet cafés are plentiful in Nice. One of the most central is

Simple fun for the kids in Jardin Albert 1er

TELEPHONING FRANCE

To call Nice from abroad, dial your own international prefix (00 in most countries) then 33 for France. The area code for southeast France, including Nice, is 04, followed by a number which is always eight digits in length. When dialling from abroad, drop the first 0, to leave 00 33 4 and the eight-digit number. When dialling Nice from anywhere in France, dial 04 and then the eight-digit number.

TELEPHONING ABROAD

To call abroad from France, dial the international access code 00, followed by the country code (UK 44, Republic of Ireland 353, USA and Canada 1, Australia 61, New Zealand 64, South Africa 27), then the area code (usually dropping the first '0' if there is one) and the local number you require.

just east of avenue Jean Médecin:

Atlanteam ⓐ 4 rue Blacas ⓣ 04 93 82 15 61 ⓦ www.atlanteam.com ⓛ 10.00–22.00 Mon–Thur, 10.00–00.00 Fri & Sat

Phone

Card-operated public phone booths are everywhere, and you can make international calls from them. You can buy phonecards (*télécartes*) at *tabacs* (newsagent/tobacconist shops sporting a red diamond sign outside), post offices and some cafés and railway stations.

Post

Post offices can be found all over Nice. The most central ones are in rue Gassin in the Old Town and on avenue Jean Médecin just south of boulevard Victor Hugo. They open 09.00–17.30 or 18.00 on weekdays and some close 12.00–14.00. They are also closed on Saturday afternoons and all day on Sundays. Stamps can be bought there or at *tabacs* (tobacconist shops). Postcards to the UK and Ireland will normally arrive in 2–3 days, taking a little longer to non-European destinations.

France has a modern and efficient postal service

ELECTRICITY

France runs on 220v with two-pin plugs. British appliances will need a simple adaptor, easily obtained at any electrical or hardware store in the centre of Nice. US and other equipment designed for 110v will need a transformer (*transformateur*).

TRAVELLERS WITH DISABILITIES

The bigger installations, such as the airport and central railway station, and many of the larger hotels, have access and facilities adapted for visitors with mobility problems. All road crossings in Nice are wheelchair-accessible, as is the central section of the beach, accessed from opposite the Jardin Albert 1er. Elsewhere the situation is less satisfactory, and the steep hills and narrow, cobbled streets of Eze and St-Paul, for instance, are unsuited to wheelchair-users. Useful organisations for advice and information include:

Association des Paralysés de France ⓐ 3 ave Antoine Véran ⓣ 04 92 07 98 00 ⓦ www.apf.asso.fr

RADAR The principal UK forum and pressure group for people with disabilities. ⓐ 12 City Forum, 250 City Road, London EC1V 8AF ⓣ (UK) 020 7250 3222 ⓦ www.radar.org.uk

SATH (Society for Accessible Travel & Hospitality) Advice for US-based travellers with disabilities. ⓐ 347 Fifth Ave, Suite 610, New York, NY 10016 ⓣ (US) 212 447 7284 ⓦ www.sath.org

TOURIST INFORMATION

Tourist offices

The Nice Convention and Visitors Bureau maintains three offices, on the seafront and at the airport and the railway station. They stock a wide range of literature and maps and have helpful staff who can make accommodation bookings and sell tickets for many attractions and events, including Carnaval.

Office du Tourisme et des Congrès ⓐ 5 prom. des Anglais ⓣ 08 92 70 74 07 ⓗ 08.00–20.00 Mon–Sat, 09.00–19.00 Sun, June–Sept; 09.00–18.00 Mon–Sat, Oct–May ⓡ Bus: 11, 52, 59, 60, 62, 94, 98, 200, 400, 500, 710, 720, 790

Office du Tourisme et des Congrès à Nice Côte d'Azur Airport–Terminal 1 ⓣ 08 92 70 74 07 ⓗ 08.00–21.00 June–Sept; 08.00–21.00 Mon–Sat, Oct–May

Office du Tourisme et des Congrès ⓐ Gare Nice-Ville, av. Thiers ⓣ 08 92 70 74 07 ⓗ 08.00–20.00 Mon–Sat, 09.00–19.00 Sun, June–Sept; 08.00–19.00 Mon–Sat, 10.00–17.00 Sun, Oct–May

Centre Régional Information Jeunesse (CRIJ) Côte d'Azur is an advice and information centre for young independent travellers in eastern central Nice, well-signposted from the middle of town. ⓐ 19 rue Gioffredo ⓣ 04 93 80 93 93 ⓦ www.crijca.fr ⓗ 10.00–18.00 Mon–Fri

Websites

The Nice tourist office website is very informative and includes a comprehensive instant accommodation booking service: ⓦ www.nicetourism.com

Additional information and listings, especially of events, can be found at: ⓦ www.nicetourisme.biz and www.nice.fr

Other useful sites include:
www.guideriviera.com (the official site of the whole Riviera)
www.cotedazur-en-fetes.com (events on the Riviera)
http://riviera.angloinfo.com (English-speaking services and information)

If you're trying to track down a business of any sort, use the French Yellow Pages site at www.pagesjaunes.fr, which also provides location maps for all its listings.

BACKGROUND READING

Nice and its environs have long been a hotbed of creative activity for artists and authors alike. To get yourself into the Côte d'Azur mindset, grab F Scott Fitzgerald's *Tender is the Night*, set on the Cap d'Antibes. Ernest Hemingway's *The Garden of Eden* takes place on the French Riviera during the 1920s. James Joyce claimed the idea for *Finnegan's Wake* came to him while visiting Nice, and in 1938, after watching a pianist perform on Cap-Ferrat, Murray Burnett wrote the play *Everybody Comes to Rick's*, on which the film *Casablanca* was based. Jean-Paul Sartre wrote *Les Chemins de la Liberté* in Saint-Tropez, and for a dose of all-American literature, Louisa May Alcott's Laurie and Amy (*Little Women*) fell in love in Nice. For fans of Henri Matisse, pick up a copy of *Chasing Matisse*, James Morgan's chronicle tracing the great artist's career through his places of residence.

Emergencies

EMERGENCY NUMBERS

The following are all national free-call emergency numbers:

Ambulance (SAMU) 15

Police (Gendarmerie) 17

Fire & first aid (Sapeurs-Pompiers) 18

To call any emergency service from a mobile phone, dial 112

MEDICAL SERVICES

Night pharmacy 7 rue Masséna 04 93 87 78 94

Hôpital St-Roch Hospital with 24-hour emergency services. Entrance on 5 rue Pierre Devoluy 04 92 03 33 75

Riviera Medical Services English-speaking doctors on call (not necessarily for emergencies). 04 93 26 12 70

SOS Dentaire Emergency dental care at night and on Sundays & public holidays. 04 97 25 72 75 or (at night) 04 93 80 77 77

EMERGENCY PHRASES

Help!	**Fire!**	**Stop!**
Au secours!	Au feu!	Stop!
Ossercoor!	*Oh fur!*	*Stop!*

Call an ambulance/a doctor/the police/the fire service!

Appelez une ambulance/un médecin/la police/les pompiers!

Ahperleh ewn ahngbewlahngss/ang medesang/lah poleess/ leh pompeeyeh!

POLICE

The Police Nationale oversee traffic and petty crime as well as dealing with more serious matters. In country districts and on motorways the Gendarmerie Nationale are the main law enforcement body. There is a mobile police post in rue Masséna and regular but low-profile patrols in the main tourist areas. An **interpreter service** (t 04 92 17 20 31 ⌚ 08.00–12.00, 14.00–18.00) is available in the central police station.

Commissariat Central de Police (Central Police Station)
a 1 av. Maréchal Foch t 04 92 17 22 22 ⌚ 24 hrs

Lost property
Police Municipale a rue Raoul Bosio t 04 97 13 44 00 ⌚ 08.30–17.00 Mon–Thur, 08.30–15.45 Fri

EMBASSIES & CONSULATES

Australian Embassy a 4 rue Jean Rey, Paris t 01 40 59 33 00
w www.france.embassy.gov.au
Canadian Consulate a 2 pl. Franklin, Nice t 04 93 92 93 22
w www.international.gc.ca
New Zealand Embassy a 7 rue Léonard da Vinci, Paris t 01 45 01 43 43
w www.nzembassy.com
Republic of Ireland Consulate a 152 blvd J-F Kennedy, Cap d'Antibes
t 04 93 61 50 63 w www.embassyofireland.fr
South African Embassy a 59 quai d'Orsay, Paris t 01 53 59 23 23
w www.afriquesud.net
UK Consulate General a 24 av. du Prado, Marseille t 04 91 15 72 10
w http://ukinfrance.fco.gov.uk
USA Consulate a 3rd Floor, 7 av. Gustave V, Nice t 04 93 88 89 55
w http://france.usembassy.gov

Editorial/project management: Lisa Plumridge
Copy editor: Monica Guy
Layout/DTP: Alison Rayner

The publishers would like to thank the following individuals and organisations for supplying their copyright photographs for this book: Ethel Davies, page 120; William Howorth, page 23; BigStockPhoto.com (John Braid, page 17; Ivan Cholakov, page 80; Rene Drouyer, pages 118–9; Pascal Fourgeau, page 47; Kersti Plehhov, pages 69 & 75; Stanley Rippel, page 117); The Leading Hotels of the World, page 89; Toufik Lerari, page 13; Tristan Rutherford, page 129; Olga Shelego/Stockxpert.com, pages 42–3; Kathryn Tomasetti, pages 5, 19, 21 & 27; Paul Medbourne and Patsy Trimnell, all others.

Send your thoughts to
books@thomascook.com

- **Found a great bar, club, shop or must-see sight that we don't feature?**
- **Like to tip us off about any information that needs a little updating?**
- **Want to tell us what you love about this handy little guidebook and more importantly how we can make it even handier?**

Then here's your chance to tell all! Send us ideas, discoveries and recommendations today and then look out for your valuable input in the next edition of this title.

Email the above address (stating the title) or write to:
pocket guides Series Editor, Thomas Cook Publishing, PO Box 227, Coningsby Road, Peterborough PE3 8SB, UK.

WHAT'S IN YOUR GUIDEBOOK?

Independent authors Impartial up-to-date information from our travel experts who meticulously source local knowledge.

Experience Thomas Cook's 165 years in the travel industry and guidebook publishing enriches every word with expertise you can trust.

Travel know-how Thomas Cook has thousands of staff working around the globe, all living and breathing travel.

Editors Travel-publishing professionals, pulling everything together to craft a perfect blend of words, pictures, maps and design.

You, the traveller We deliver a practical, no-nonsense approach to information, geared to how you really use it.

Useful phrases

English	French	*Approx pronunciation*
	BASICS	
Yes	Oui	*Wee*
No	Non	*Nawng*
Please	S'il vous plaît	*Seel voo pleh*
Thank you	Merci	*Mehrsee*
Hello	Bonjour	*Bawngzhoor*
Goodbye	Au revoir	*Aw revwahr*
Excuse me	Excusez-moi	*Ekskeweh mwah*
Sorry	Désolé(e)	*Dehzoleh*
That's okay	Ça va	*Sahr vahr*
I don't speak French	Je ne parle pas français	*Zher ner pahrl pah frahngsay*
Do you speak English?	Parlez-vous anglais?	*Pahrlay-voo ahnglay?*
Good morning	Bonjour	*Bawng-zhoor*
Good afternoon	Bonjour	*Bawng-zhoor*
Good evening	Bonsoir	*Bawng-swah*
Goodnight	Bonne nuit	*Bun nwee*
My name is ...	Je m'appelle ...	*Zher mahpehl ...*
	NUMBERS	
One	Un/Une	*Uhn/Oon*
Two	Deux	*Dur*
Three	Trois	*Trwah*
Four	Quatre	*Kahtr*
Five	Cinq	*Sank*
Six	Six	*Seess*
Seven	Sept	*Seht*
Eight	Huit	*Weet*
Nine	Neuf	*Nurf*
Ten	Dix	*Deess*
Twenty	Vingt	*Vang*
Fifty	Cinquante	*Sangkahnt*
One hundred	Cent	*Sohn*
	SIGNS & NOTICES	
Airport	Aéroport	*Ahehrohpohr*
Rail station/Platform	Gare/Quai	*Gahr/Kay*
Smoking/Non-smoking	Fumeurs/Non fumeurs	*Foomurh/Nawng foomurh*
Toilets	Toilettes	*Twahlayt*
Ladies/Gentlemen	Femmes/Hommes	*Fam/Ommh*
Bus	Bus	*Boos*